Weaving with Paper
I0815818

WEAVING WITH PAPER

30 Projects to Expand Your Creativity
with Inventive Techniques, Intriguing Prompts, and Inspiring Works of Art

HELEN HIEBERT

Storey Publishing

The mission of Storey Publishing is to serve our customers by publishing practical information that encourages personal independence in harmony with the environment.

EDITED BY Kristen Hewitt
ART DIRECTION AND BOOK DESIGN BY Bredna Lago
TEXT PRODUCTION BY Jennifer Jepson Smith

COVER PHOTOGRAPHY BY Mars Vilaubi © Storey Publishing, except spine © Naomi J. Kendall
INTERIOR PHOTOGRAPHY BY Mars Vilaubi © Storey Publishing
ADDITIONAL PHOTOGRAPHY BY © Amanda J. Thackray, 50–51; American Folk Art Museum/Art Resource, NY, 23 t.; © Audrey L. Pinto, 27; Courtesy of the author, 8–9; © Carole Kunstadt, 198–199; Dorothy McGuinness, 200–201; Courtesy of Galen Gibson-Cornell, 192–195; © Hollie Chastain, 190–191; © Janice McDonald, 65; © Julie VonDerVellen, 204–205; Courtesy of Karen Krieger, 143 b.; Mary Balzer Buskirk, Untitled (shield), c. 1968, 36"×24", wool, nylon, and twigs © copyright estate of Mary Balzer Buskirk, courtesy of the Buskirk family, 23 b.; © Naomi J. Kendall, 196–197; © rhiannon skye tafoya, 202–203; Stefan Hagen, courtesy of Aimee Lee, 18; Courtesy of Susan J. Byrd, 17; © Susan Kristoferson, 208; Takeshi Yamamoto; @Takashi Yamamoto; Courtesy of Hiroko Karuno, 16; © Therese Zemlin, 206–207; Virginia Museum of Fine Arts, Richmond. Funds provided by Margaret A. and C. Boyd Clarke and Mareke Schiller, 2021.191

Storey Publishing
210 MASS MoCA Way
North Adams, MA 01247
storey.com

Storey Publishing is an imprint of Workman Publishing, a division of Hachette Book Group, Inc., 1290 Avenue of the Americas, New York, NY 10104. The Storey Publishing name and logo are registered trademarks of Hachette Book Group, Inc.

ISBNs: 978-1-63586-796-1 (paperback);
978-1-63586-819-7 (ebook)

Printed in China by R. R. Donnelley on paper from responsible sources
10 9 8 7 6 5 4 3 2 1

APS

Library of Congress Cataloging-in-Publication Data on file

To Friedrich Froebel,
who developed a series of educational gifts
for children in the eighteenth century—
number 14 was paper weaving.
Discovering your work has
opened so many doors for me.

And to participants in my Paper Weaving
and Weave Through Winter (WTW) online classes.
I have learned more than I can express from you—
about paper weaving techniques, the daily practice,
and challenging myself. It has been an honor to work
and grow with you.

Contents

Introduction

I cut diagonal strips (left) and curved strips (right) to create these two lamps in the early 1990s.

I have a vague memory of weaving strips of construction paper in elementary school—did you weave them, too? My interest in this practice was rekindled when I started working with paper in college. First, I discovered a unique Japanese style of pop-ups called "origamic architecture." Then, shortly after graduating, I visited Japan and was inspired by the paper and wood shoji screens (room dividers) and the way that light filtered through the paper. I began teaching myself how to construct shoji screens and paper lampshades and experimenting with ways to enhance the paper with light—layering, piercing holes, and even making my own paper with watermarks.

Sometime in my twenties, I recalled that early paper weaving from childhood, and I created two lamps with woven shades. I was surprised (and disappointed) when the result wasn't what I expected. The light blurred the over/under weaving pattern, so that the woven paper looked homogeneous when backlit. There were a couple of interesting effects, however: The slits (or gaps) between the woven segments did let light through, and the weaving looked different when the lamps were turned on (the papers blended) as opposed to when they were off (the papers had the familiar woven checkerboard pattern).

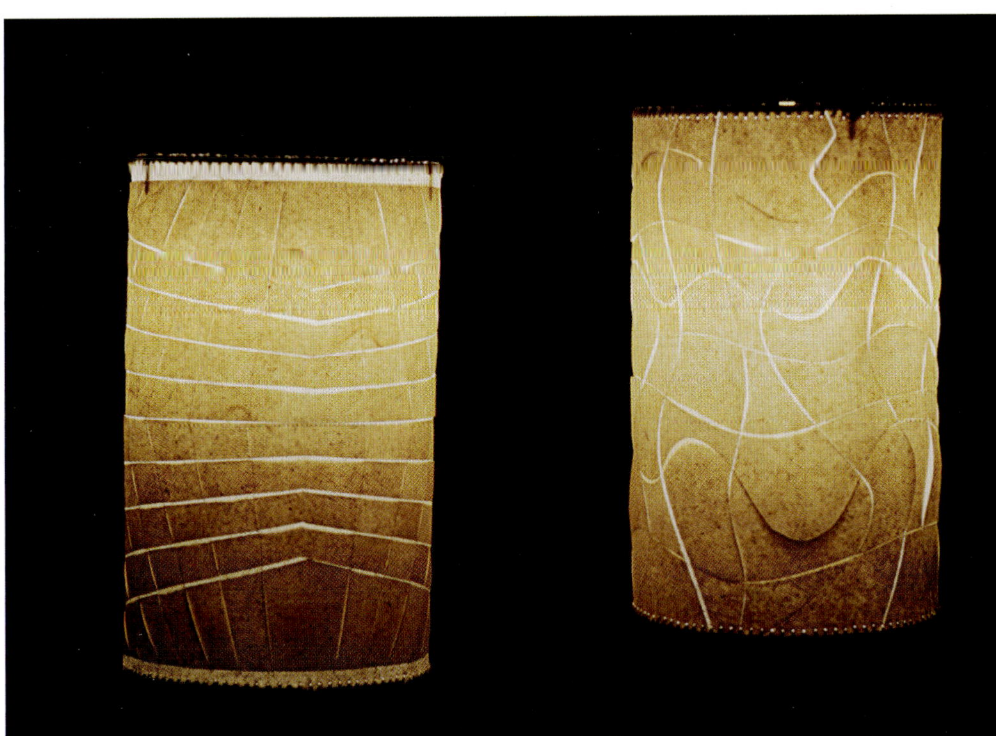

When I illuminated these lamps, I was surprised that the paper colors blended, but I was intrigued by how the slits between the woven strips created an interesting effect.

I embarked on a quest to find a way to differentiate between those woven layers, and I came up with the idea of cutting "windows" in one of the layers, which resulted in the effect I was looking for!

My work with paper continued, but I didn't weave paper again for several years. When my family moved to Colorado in 2012, my husband had a job (which precipitated the move), my kids were in middle school, and I had to figure out how to establish myself in a new community.

I started two initiatives in 2013: I began *The Sunday Paper Blog* (a weekly blog that continues to this day), and I launched my own 100-Day Project, creating 100 weavings over the last 100 days of that year. This was a challenge to myself, a call to action. As an artist, I found myself getting sidetracked with bookkeeping, marketing, writing grant proposals . . . you name it! The 100-Day Project gave me a focus to create something new daily, and it was rewarding in so many ways: It reignited a creative spark and allowed me to explore various papers, and, as someone who doesn't like doing repetitive tasks, this daily practice propelled me to push the boundaries of paper weaving because I was determined to do something different each day. My weekly blog about the project even garnered unexpected attention (and sales) from my online community.

In 2017, I began teaching online, and in 2019, I turned that 100-day weaving project into an online class called Weave Through Winter.

My daily practice propelled me to push the boundaries of paper weaving because I was determined to do something different every day.

Early in my career, I was looking for a way to reveal light between layers of woven paper and discovered a method of cutting "windows."

Cutting windows into one layer of paper creates a dramatic effect when a paper weaving is illuminated.

Ever since, I have run this class annually during the month of February (winter here in the United States) and shortened it to one month. I teach basic paper weaving principles in four weekly lessons, and participants (including me) share what we create in an online classroom, as we participate in a daily practice.

This book grew out of that online class. I learned so much through my 100-Day Project, not only about weaving, but about paper itself, my work ethic, and letting go of the drive for perfection. The community component that came out of the course enhanced my accountability, my anticipation of how others would respond to daily prompts (a word of the day meant to spark ideas and create a unifying challenge for the group), my enjoyment of sharing my own weavings, and my excitement at seeing the weavings of others. The participants echoed those sentiments.

I've taken the gems from Weave Through Winter and turned them into this paper weaving journey for you.

Weaving a Way Forward: The Möbius Map

Weaving is a metaphor for so many things in life. When I create art, it is intertwined with the questions I ponder in the spaces I inhabit as an artist, as a family member, in the various communities I belong to, and on our planet. *Möbius Map* weaves together maps and visions for the world that I collected from the paper community. I sent out a call for 1"-wide map strips and received town, city, country, continent, and world maps featuring various types of navigation aids: aeronautical, trail, migration pattern, tide, and current. Each contributor included a handwritten vision for the world on the back of their map strip, in a variety of languages. The maps are woven together, rendering the visions only partly visible, a metaphor for how hard it is to come to global understanding.

Among the "visions" I received:

- Seeing a world that embraces diversity
- Safety for the next generation
- Putting women on the map
- Economic equity across the globe

As I wove the maps together, I pondered how we use maps—to help us find our way and make sense of our world. As the weaving grew, I twisted the length of the woven maps into a Möbius strip—an infinite loop. If you follow the crocheted strand that is woven through the centerline of the piece, you end up where you started. There is no front or back, top or bottom. We humans are all on this wild ride, circling through time and space together. It is my hope that we will gain empathy for what others are facing—by sharing and reading each other's visions—and sustain our planet as we journey into the future.

A NOTE ABOUT MY PERSPECTIVE

I am an artist, not an art historian, so this book delves into what I have discovered about paper weaving over the years. No doubt there are aspects of this amazing craft that I haven't come across (yet). I look forward to continuing to find examples of weavings from history, other cultures, and contemporary artists that illustrate how paper weaving has enhanced our world through the millennia.

Helpful Notes

Here are a few things to keep in mind as you read this book.

Terminology

Paper weaving is a relatively new craft, so I have developed a few paper weaving terms of my own, including *partial warp* and *strip weaving*. Some of these terms stem from traditional cloth weaving. These terms are italicized when they are first introduced, and you'll find a paper weaving glossary on page 209.

Paper Names

There isn't a standard convention for paper names. Some papers are named for their fiber content (e.g., Thai unryu), others are referred to by color or look (e.g., hand-marbled paper: funky stone), while others are named for the technique used to create them (e.g., momigami, which is kneaded/crumpled paper). Other characteristics influence paper names, such as the region or country where they were made or the name of the maker. In addition, two suppliers might carry the same paper by different names. For these reasons, I have included details that I feel are relevant to help guide you in choosing papers, but I haven't listed specific papers to use for projects by name (though you'll find papers used in the works featured throughout the book in the back matter). There are also several paper suppliers listed in the resources (page 210).

Measurements

Measurements in the main text are expressed in imperial, rather than metric, form: in inches, rather than centimeters or millimeters. For readers who prefer to use metric measurements, I've included a metric conversion chart toward the end of the book (see page 210), with metric conversion ratios.

Dimensions

Artwork measurements are listed as height × width, or height × width × depth for sculptural works. Both artwork and paper sizes are listed using this convention.

Templates

There are a few downloadable templates (see page 210 for link) to assist you in mastering some of the weaving structures in Chapter 5.

1
EXPLORING THE ORIGINS

Weaving has a long history that has developed over millennia, growing and changing with humans' many technological innovations. Paper weaving is a more recent invention, and by exploring the history of weaving, we can see its impact on the craft of paper weaving today.

Habit is a cable. We weave a thread of it every day, and at last we cannot break it.

—**Horace Mann**, father of American education

Early Cloth Weaving

Weaving dates back to early human history. Our ancestors twisted plant and animal fibers together to make thread and string, which they wove into textiles, and wove baskets with pliable plant materials, some resembling strips of paper. Paper weaving seems to have originated in Germany in the 1700s, when Friedrich Froebel developed a set of "gifts" for kindergarten children, one of which was paper weaving.

As with many crafts, it is difficult to trace the specific origins of traditional cloth weaving, but we know that early humans made thread and string—which they eventually spun by hand and later by machine—that they twisted onto spools and into skeins. Around the fifth century BCE, looms were developed, ranging from warps hanging in tree branches to simple wooden frames and backstrap looms that were easy to transport. Threads were woven into textiles and other functional objects.

Cloth weaving was mechanized with the development of steam- and water-powered looms during the Industrial Revolution, which began in the 1700s. The Jacquard machine (developed in the early 1800s in France) was a revolutionary device that used a punch-card mechanism to guide the mechanical weaving process and is the precursor to modern computer science. Throughout history—and still today—weavers have been developing new and innovative weaving methods.

In the Japanese paper weaving tradition of shifu, handmade papers are spun into skeins of thread, such as these made by Hiroko Karuno, to be woven into kimonos.

Early Paper Weaving

There is a paper weaving tradition in Japan called shifu (in Japanese, *shi* means "paper" and *fu* means "cloth"). Handmade bark papers (called kigami) were laboriously harvested, processed, spun into thread called kami-ito (*kami* means "paper" and *ito* means "thread"), and then woven into paper cloth. This cloth was turned into paper garments, which were most popular during the Edo period in the seventeenth century.

Hiroko Karuno is a self-taught contemporary maker who uses the purest Japanese artist-made paper to create kami-ito, cutting it with precision and spinning it to the appropriate fineness for warp and weft. She then weaves lengths of shifu to the dimensions required to make a kimono.

The Art of Shifu: Weaving Paper Kimonos

In 1984, Susan Byrd went to Japan to study the Japanese paper called washi, and while there, she met the esteemed shifu weaver Sadako Sakurai, with whom she later studied. In 2013, her book *A Song of Praise for Shifu* was published to help preserve the traditional craft of shifu. Susan continues to make her own shifu as well as mentor others interested in learning to make a woven paper cloth that is both washable and wearable. Susan wove this garment during her stay at Mrs. Sakurai's home. It was her first-ever weaving, and Mrs. Sakurai commented that the stripes reflected a Western design.

Basket Weaving

Other materials have been woven for centuries—sticks were loosely woven to create fences and walls, and basket weaving developed around the world as our ancestors used grasses, bark, roots, and other plant materials to weave vessels to gather, store, cook, and serve food. Cane strips (from the fast-growing stem or trunk of the rattan palm) have been used in weaving objects since ancient times, originating as basket material and evolving into furniture (most common today are caned chair seats).

In Korea, hanji (paper) was cut into strips and twisted into cords. Basketry techniques were used to weave the cords into a variety of useful objects, such as shoes, quivers, brush holders, baskets, vessels, bags, purses, and lanterns.

Traditional Indigenous basket-weaving techniques have also sparked contemporary interest in paper weaving. Artists from several tribes incorporate paper into their work. Shan Goshorn, a member of the Eastern Band of Cherokee, studied the intricate basket-weaving techniques and structures of her forebears in museums, since nobody in her immediate family was a weaver. She wove political, social, and cultural commentary into her own work, in both words and images.

Aimee Lee, a paper artist and author of *Hanji Unfurled*, studied the traditional craft of jiseung (paper weaving) with Na Seo-hwan, a third-generation jiseung master. Aimee creates her own paper sculptures using the technique she learned from her mentor.

Squaw is the last work Shan Goshorn completed before her passing in 2018; it was inspired by the Venus de Milo, an iconic symbol of female beauty. Calling this piece *Squaw* juxtaposes the Western ideal of beauty against a pejorative used to reduce Native American women to disposable sexual commodities. *Squaw* serves as a catalyst for much-needed conversations on why Native American women suffer disproportionately higher rates of violence than non-Native women and the judicial system's reluctance to prosecute these crimes.

Paper Weaving in School

Nineteenth-century German educator Friedrich Froebel studied pedagogy at the Frankfurt Model School, where he met Johann Heinrich Pestalozzi in 1805. Pestalozzi favored hands-on activities over memorization and recitation, which were popular at the time, and paper weaving was one such activity. Froebel, who went on to invent kindergarten in Germany, developed a set of "gifts" for children, and the fourteenth gift was paper weaving. Froebel's educational model spread widely (he started a college for the training of "kindergartners," as kindergarten teachers were called) and is most likely the basis for the paper weavings many of us did in elementary school. Today you can find historic weaving albums featuring incredible weavings made with ⅛" to ¼" paper strips (see page 20).

In my research, I stumbled across a few old books for teachers on how to teach paper weaving and basket weaving. One such book, *Varied Occupations in Weaving* (1901; see Suggested Reading, page 211), was written by Louisa Walker, headmistress of the Fleet Road Board School in Hampstead, England, who received her training in Froebelian principles.

The *Froebel Album* contains 24 original paper weaving designs and was probably used for display in a classroom to inspire children. The weavings are mounted on board pages that are bound like an accordion, allowing the weavings to be stretched out for display and then folded up and enclosed in the book cover.

Froebel's gifts made their way to America, perhaps through the Prang Educational Company, which is still in business today. The company was founded in 1882 by Louis Prang, who believed that art played a vital role in fostering imagination and independent expression especially in children. A series called *Text Books of Art Education* (1904) was published by Prang and Book II includes a couple of simple paper weavings.

The toy company Milton Bradley produced paper weaving kits between 1880 and 1900 that were available for kindergarten teachers

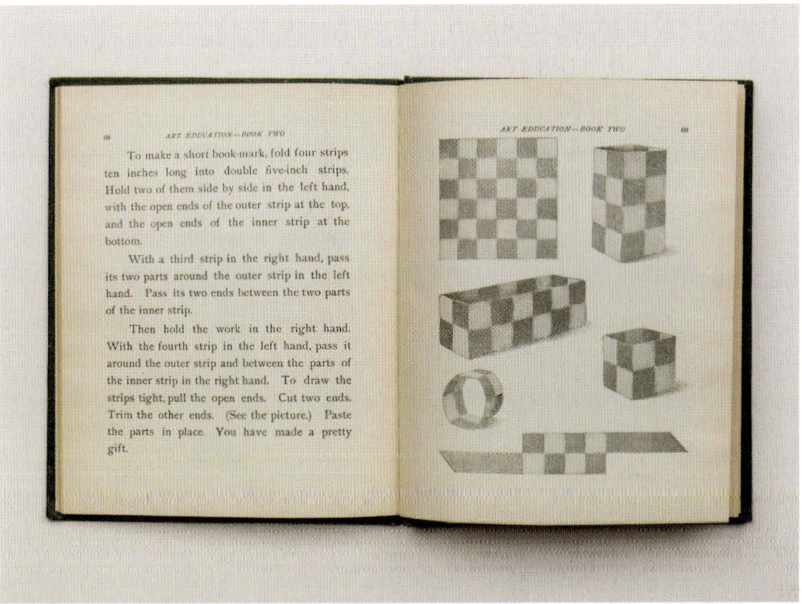

68 ART EDUCATION—BOOK TWO

To make a short book-mark, fold four strips ten inches long into double five-inch strips. Hold two of them side by side in the left hand, with the open ends of the outer strip at the top, and the open ends of the inner strip at the bottom.

With a third strip in the right hand, pass its two parts around the outer strip in the left hand. Pass its two ends between the two parts of the inner strip.

Then hold the work in the right hand. With the fourth strip in the left hand, pass it around the outer strip and between the parts of the inner strip in the right hand. To draw the strips tight, pull the open ends. Cut two ends. Trim the other ends. (See the picture.) Paste the parts in place. You have made a pretty gift.

ART EDUCATION—BOOK TWO 69

Text Books of Art Education, Book II, Second Year, 1904, has a couple of pages that show a unique way of weaving folded strips of paper.

This paper weaving kit by Pomegranate Communications seems to be a new version of the original Milton Bradley kit. I've seen pictures of an older kit that includes a weaving tool.

to use with their students. With pre-slit mats, colored strips, and a flat tin "needle" (I will refer to this as a weaving tool), children learned counting, progression, method, composition, planning, and creativity by weaving paper. Norman Brosterman's book *Inventing Kindergarten* is a wonderful resource about Friedrich Froebel's gifts to children, and there are several pages dedicated to paper weaving, including a mention of Frank Lloyd Wright's mother, Anna, who introduced him to Froebel's gifts as a child.

In the mid-1860s, Danish author Hans Christian Andersen created a woven paper "basket" for a friend. Perhaps he went to a Froebel-inspired kindergarten? His clever design, which involves weaving two folded pieces of paper together, has become a classic Christmas ornament found throughout Scandinavia. Danish artists Anna and Lena Schepper feature many contemporary designs on their website and in their book *The Art of Paper Weaving: 46 Colorful, Dimensional Projects*.

Somewhere along the way, paper weaving seems to have almost died out. In some European countries, however, you can still purchase sets of weaving tools. And I learned to weave that basic place mat in elementary school.

Modern Weaving

In my childhood home in the 1970s, we had a contemporary tapestry wall hanging that had been created by my father's cousin, Mary Balzer Buskirk, an American textile artist known for being part of the mid-century modern movement. The weaving incorporated sticks, mixed fibers, and variations in the *weaving structure*. I can't help but think that the piece, created outside of the applied textile tradition, influenced my interest in materials (and weaving).

Artists in the 1960s took weaving beyond the loom and off the wall, allowing tapestry to become sculpture.

Several other artists working in the 1960s—Lenore Tawney, Sheila Hicks, Anni Albers, and Ruth Asawa, to name just a few—gained notoriety for weaving unusual materials. They also took weaving beyond the loom and off the wall, and tapestry became sculpture, which was innovative at the time. These women all have a connection to the Bauhaus, the groundbreaking early twentieth-century German art school that combined crafts and the fine arts, but none of them wove paper to my knowledge, although students of Albers's husband (Josef Albers) were experimenting with paper in other ways. A handful of artists, also with Bauhaus connections, explored paper weaving around that time, among them Gertrud Goldschmidt (aka Gego) and Naum Gabo.

Paper weaving has blossomed since the 1990s, and in the last chapter of this book, I spotlight a range of works by eight professional artists who are currently weaving paper.

During the nineteenth century, cut-out paper hearts and hands were exchanged as tokens of love, friendship, and gestures of regard all year long. This piece is in the collection of the American Folk Art Museum in New York City.

This weaving by Mary Balzer Buskirk features a shield shape and areas of bound warp that create transparencies. It is pulled in at the bottom by interweaving warp through warp. As Mary's estate explains, "The composition is abstract with a landscape derivation."

2
TOOLS & MATERIALS

The great thing about paper weaving is that the supplies you need are minimal. You can weave almost any paper, and once you master the basics, you can explore the wide world of papers that are available for purchase. You won't need much in terms of equipment, either—but there are a few specialized tools you may wish to acquire.

> If art is the bridge between what you see in your mind and what the world sees, then skill is how you build that bridge.
>
> —**Twyla Tharp**, dancer, choreographer, and author of *The Creative Habit*

Paper (Of Course!)

Start your paper stash by looking at your junk mail and in your recycling bin—you can weave all kinds of papers, from wrapping paper, cards, announcements, and catalogs to maps, old book and dictionary pages, calendars, and more. A mix of commercial papers from suppliers (see Resources, page 210) and found papers will make your weavings unique and interesting. I have a hunch that you'll start seeing interesting papers everywhere.

I like to think of finding papers as a treasure hunt! Here are some types of paper you might enjoy weaving:

- Maps
- Calendar pages
- Photocopies
- Scanned images printed on paper
- Security envelopes
- Photographs (make a photocopy if you want to preserve the original)
- Postcards
- Stamps
- Book pages
- Sheet music
- Prints or old artwork
- Graph paper
- Pre-cut strips, such as Froebel star strips and quilling strips (available online)

You can also integrate other flat items into your weavings:

- Ribbon
- Thin, pliable bark
- Tree needles
- Plastic netting
- Raffia

You can weave all kinds of papers into your projects, such as calendar pages, maps, stamps, junk mail, and more.

CHOOSING YOUR PAPERS

Here's what I look for in the papers I weave, but I encourage you to experiment. There isn't a paper that's exactly right, which means there are lots of good possibilities out there. You'll begin to discover your favorite papers on your own weaving journey.

Weight/thickness/stiffness: Paper thickness is described in weight. I find that thin papers with some body (such as magazine pages) weave best. Papers that are thicker (think of a stiff paperback cover) are not flexible enough in most situations, and papers that are too thin (tissue paper) can wrinkle or tear and often bunch up when you try to weave them. And remember this simple but important tip to avoid frustration:

> *Weaving two papers that are similar in weight is best—if you try weaving a thin paper into a thick paper, or vice versa, you can run into trouble.*

The Joys of Recycling

Audrey L. Pinto was suffering from COVID-19 shutdown syndrome when she signed up to participate in Weave Through Winter in 2021. The course helped her focus, and afterward, she decided to apply for the low-residency MFA program at Lesley University. While there, she developed a body of paper weavings and received her degree in 2024. Audrey utilized recycled materials that were gifted to her or fibers that she knew were reclaimed. Each woven strip of paper represents a memory or thought, and each image of a woman or object (from recycled magazine pages) is carefully hidden within the weaving, representing the universal experience of women having to navigate between visibility and invisibility, hiding and revealing, remaining silent or speaking out—always cognizant of thoughts and feelings diminished and marginalized by societal norms that demand conformity.

Audrey Pinto used recycled and reclaimed magazine covers, honeycomb packing paper, sari silk threads and ribbons, beads, wires, and sisal. Her weaving is suspended from wrapped tree branches.

Size: I recommend starting small to gain experience, but there are no limits.

Texture: Papers with different textures give your weaving surface personality and create more dimension in your weaving. Try weaving something very textured, like sandpaper, with something smooth, or crinkle some of your paper strips and then flatten them. You can also incorporate textured nonpaper items like ribbon, raffia, or starched fabric into your weavings. Keep in mind that textured papers might be trickier to weave.

Add texture to your weaving by incorporating items such as packing materials, crumpled or folded papers, and sandpaper.

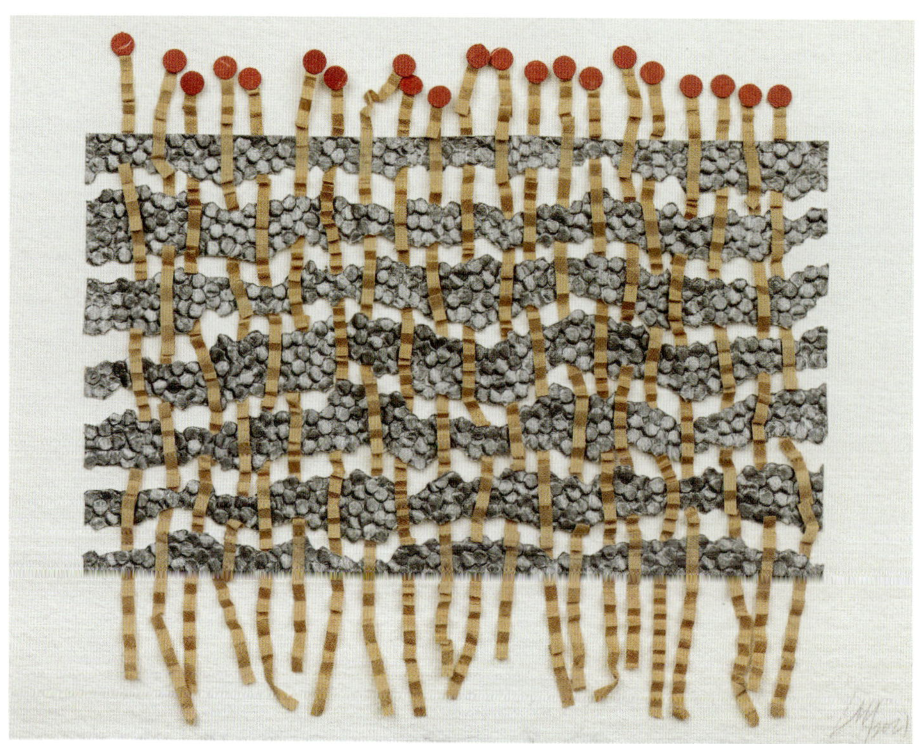

Lisa Merkin's weaving *Garden* incorporates textured flower "roots" woven between strips of embossed paper "gravel."

Opacity/transparency: Adding a layer of translucent paper will give your weaving more depth. By showing what's underneath, you also create a sense of history. Try weaving opaque and translucent papers together.

Color: Use contrasting, coordinated, similar, or unusual color combinations in your weaving. Integrate wild or organic colors. Weave in one color to highlight the weaving structure, weave color into black and white, or try creating the same weaving using two different color combinations.

In *Egg Basket* I used translucent pleated, artist-made abaca paper with a decorative paper to add depth.

Imagery: Use photos (print out digital copies on unique papers or make a copy of any original you don't want to destroy) or look for images in magazines or old books. Several websites offer free images in a variety of categories, with a paid option to upgrade (see Resources, page 210).

In *Smock,* I wove a colorful, patterned paper into a black-and-white image of one of my baby pictures.

Copyright Infringement

You need to consider issues involving copyright if you use images that are not your own. You must be mindful of copyright if you will be showing or selling your work. However, if your work is solely for personal use, copyright may not be an issue. The rule is that if an image isn't your original work, either don't use it or obtain permission from the owner or creator of the copyrighted material. All works published in the United States before 1924 are in the public domain, so you can use them without any legal consequence. And you can look up guidelines for copyright on more recent work at copyright.gov.

Other Materials

Adhesives: I like to use PVA glue, which is an archival white glue available from fine art supply stores and bookbinding suppliers, but you can use any white glue. Glue sticks may work for you, but they are not as permanent. I love double-sided tape, but you'll usually have to adhere a lot of spots on paper weavings, so applying tape can get tedious. The glue pen makes applying glue to the ends of strips a breeze—you just draw it on! For situations where you wish to tack down a large area and avoid moisture (from glue), try using a sheet adhesive. I often use a low-tack tape for holding things in place as I weave.

Flexible plastic place mat: This is key for cutting windows between layers of woven paper. You can find thin, flexible kitchen place mats or cutting

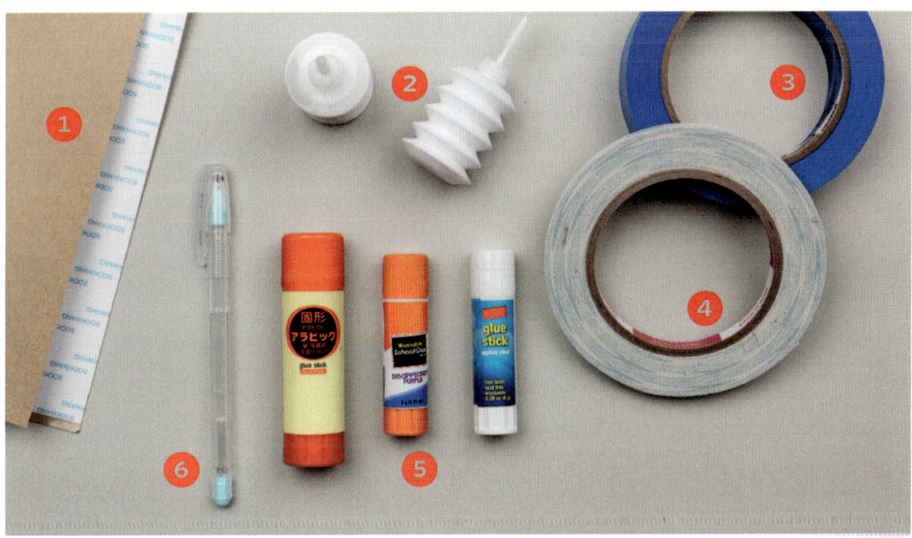

Clockwise from left: (1) sheet adhesive, (2) accordion squeeze glue applicator, (3) low-tack tape, (4) double-sided tape, (5) glue sticks, (6) glue pen

Use flexible plastic mats, cut to different shapes and sizes, to cut between layers of woven paper.

mats at grocery or dollar stores. You only need a small piece, but it will wear out over time. Upcycling is a great option—you can utilize flat pieces of milk cartons, milk jugs, or yogurt containers. You will find this type of thin plastic elsewhere, too—for example, as a protective cover on some spiral-bound notebooks.

Scrap paper: I place scrap paper underneath my weavings when gluing—newsprint works well for this purpose. Waxed paper and freezer paper are good alternatives, and they have nonstick surfaces.

Tools

- Pencil (1)
- Ruler (12"–18"): I like metal rulers for cutting, plus plastic see-through gridded rulers for measuring same-size strips (2)
- Scissors (3)
- Cutting mat (4) + craft knife (5) *OR* rotary cutter (6) + quilting ruler (7)
- Eraser (8)
- Glue brushes (9)

It's helpful to have an assortment of pencils, scissors, rulers, and cutting tools to create different shapes and styles of strips. Experiment and see which tools work best for you.

Other Useful Items

- **Accordion squeeze glue applicator (1):** This is my favorite gluing tool, and I usually use it in combination with a small glue brush.
- **Circle cutter (2):** You can draw a circle with a compass and cut it by hand, but a circle cutter makes for almost-perfect circles. I say *almost* because it takes time to get the hang of using circle cutters, and they vary widely in terms of quality.
- **Condiment cup with lid (3):** This is perfect for small amounts of white glue.
- **Cut-resistant glove:** If you're worried about cutting yourself when using a craft knife, wear a kitchen glove on your nondominant hand.
- **Electronic cutting machine:** This makes intricate cutting more precise and much faster than cutting by hand.
- **Light box (4):** This makes tracing a breeze; you can use it to check the tightness of your weaving; and if you're cutting windows to let light through woven layers, you can set your weaving on a light box to view your progress. I like the thin, inexpensive, LED-powered light boxes.
- **Metal triangle (5):** This will often come in handy.
- **Pasta machines:** These allow you to cut multiple thin strips in a flash.
- **Portable paper trimmer (6):** This is inexpensive and makes cutting strips so much faster.
- **Tracing paper:** I use this to determine placement for shaped weavings and to sketch ideas for strip shapes.
- **Tweezers (7):** These can come in handy, and I find that pointy tips are best for grabbing paper.
- **Weaving tools (8):** These make pulling paper through weaving slits simple.

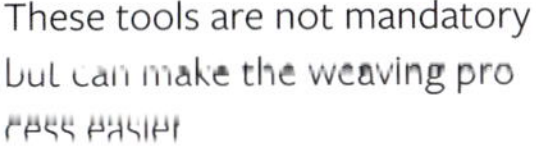
These tools are not mandatory but can make the weaving process easier.

3

LEARNING THE BASICS & DEVELOPING YOUR DESIGN EYE

In this chapter you'll learn about techniques that apply to most paper weavings, from weaving fundamentals to methods for finishing off projects. You'll also explore a variety of weaving structures and discover how to integrate design principles into your weavings.

The artist is a receptacle for emotions that come from all over the place: from the sky, from the earth, from a scrap of paper, from a passing shape, from a spider's web.

—**Pablo Picasso**, twentieth-century artist

Try making a series of weaving samples as a reference tool and place them in a sample book like this.

Fundamentals of Paper Weaving

Here are some basic weaving techniques that you'll use frequently on your paper weaving journey.

We'll begin with *strip weaving* (cutting strips and weaving them together), progress to weaving into a *partial warp*, and then advance to weaving *weft strips* into a *paper warp* or *paper loom*. Along the way, we'll add curves and windows and learn some finishing techniques.

STRIP WEAVING

Traditional cloth weaving on a handloom consists of a *warp*, which is composed of the vertical set of yarns that are fastened to the loom, and a *weft*, the horizontal yarn that is wound onto a shuttle and gets woven over and under the warp yarns.

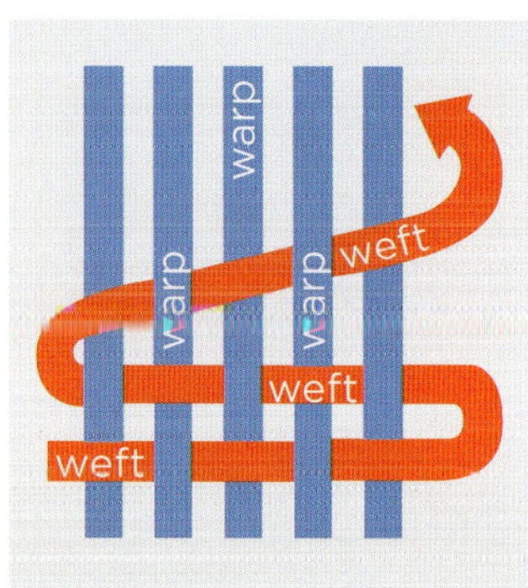

In paper strip weaving, the warp and weft are interchangeable, because the pieces are all individual strips. For the sake of clarity, I will use the term *warp* to refer to vertical strips and *weft* to refer to horizontal strips (unless otherwise noted).

How to Cut and Weave Your Strips

1. Use a cutting tool and a straightedge (a gridded quilting ruler and rotary cutter; a metal ruler, craft knife, and cutting mat; or a portable paper cutter) to cut two 6" squares of paper into six 1" strips. It's good practice to keep your strips in order—you'll need one vertical set and one horizontal set. I like to keep my strips on my cutting mat, so I can move the mat around while keeping the strips in place.
2. Line up your warp strips so that they resemble the original square of paper, and carefully weave the top weft strip into the warp: over/under/over/under/over/under.
3. Weave the second weft strip underneath the first in the opposite pattern: under/over/under/over/under/over.
4. Continue weaving weft strips in the pattern established in steps 2 and 3.
5. Weave in the last strip and make any desired adjustments.

This over/under, under/over structure is called *plain weave.*

Tightening Your Weave

As you weave, you will need to tighten up the weaving by pushing the strips as close together as you can. Use the tip of your cutting knife or the eraser on a pencil to help push your strips together (as shown in the photo for step 4, below).

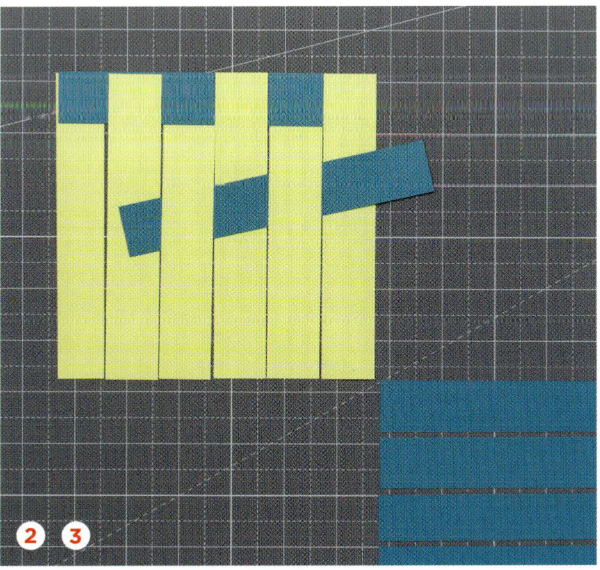

Securing Your Strips

Try these helpful tips for keeping your strips from moving around while you're weaving.

- Use removable tape to tack down the edges of one set of strips. Some tapes do not come off easily and will tear your paper—I recommend testing the tape on the paper to make sure it will release. You can touch the tape to your clothing to make it a bit less sticky. Or, if you make your strips slightly longer, you can cut off the taped edge after weaving (1).
- Tack/pin your strips into a piece of foam core, cork board, or Styrofoam (see, for an example, Weaving 21 on page 137).
- Use weights to hold your strips in place, moving the weights around as you weave.

FINISHING TOUCHES

These finishing touches apply to all weaving techniques. Once I have finished a weaving, I almost always glue the ends, and if strips are askew, I trim the edges.

Gluing the Ends

In most cases, once you complete a weaving, you'll glue the ends down to keep the pieces in place. Here's how.

1. Place your weaving on top of a piece of scrap paper or on a surface you can easily wipe clean.
2. Lift the end of a strip that needs to be glued and squirt a thin bead of glue onto the back side of the very end of the strip, using a small glue applicator and a brush (or just a brush).
3. Brush the glue out to the edge, so that it coats the entire end of the strip and there aren't any globs.
4. Lay the end of the strip down and press it to adhere.
5. Repeat to adhere all loose ends, then flip your weaving over and glue the loose ends on the other side of your weaving.

Note: I glue only the very edges of the strip ends, in case I decide to cut windows. We're not there yet—windows come later in the journey (see page 48).

Trimming the Edges

It is often difficult to get the edges of a weaving lined up perfectly due to *take-up*. Use a ruler and a cutting knife to trim uneven edges—work carefully, because cutting through uneven layers can be tricky.

Glue the ends of the strips down.

Trim the edges.

10 STRIP WEAVING VARIATIONS

Here are 10 design decisions that can influence the look of your strip weavings. This is just a start—I hope you will add to this list.

Vary the strip widths.

Weave curved strips with straight strips.

Weave curved strips into curved strips.

Cut the warp and weft strips together in the same pattern. After cutting, carefully separate them but keep them in order. Turn one set 90 degrees and then weave them together.

Tear your strips or used deckle-edge scissors to create unique edges.

Vary the strip lengths.

Leave space between the strips.

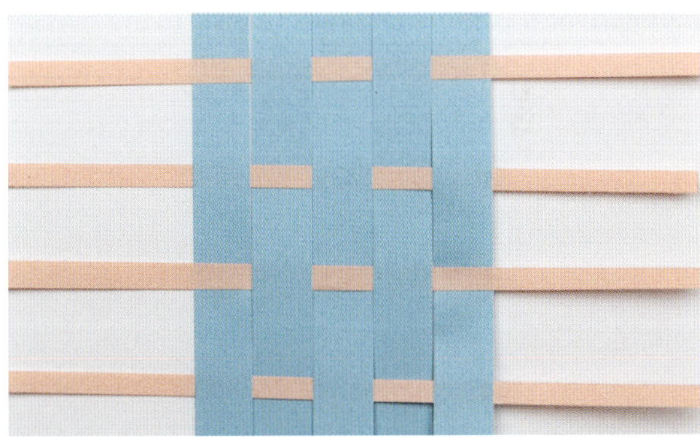

Leave space between the warp *or* the weft strips.

Angle your warp and/or weft strips.

Weave straight strips into diagonal strips.

EXPLORING THE WEAVING STRUCTURE

Many traditional and contemporary weaving structures can be found in books, online, and in the real world. Following are a few ways to find patterns that will work for weaving paper. I also encourage you to look for inspiration in fabrics, the world of fashion, printed materials, architecture, and even nature.

- Friedrich Froebel (see page 19) came up with weaving structures for kindergarten teachers to share with students. A search online for "Froebel and paper weaving" will lead to many results. (Read more about Froebel and his "gifts" in Norman Brosterman's book *Inventing Kindergarten*; see Suggested Reading, page 211.)
- People around the world have been weaving a variety of materials for centuries. Look for traditional designs from different cultures in books, online, and perhaps in your linen closet.
- Finally, don't forget that you can design your own weaving structure (freehand or on graph paper).

Kristi Galbraith used a Diné rug pattern for inspiration and drafted her weaving structure on graph paper. She added a few collage elements to complete the pattern.

THE PARTIAL WARP

A *partial warp* (or *partial loom*) is created when part of the warp paper is left uncut. This makes weaving in the weft strips easier because one edge of the warp paper is secured.

How to Weave with a Partial Warp

1. Cut slits in the warp sheet, beginning midsheet and extending down through the bottom edge. This is the partial warp/loom.
2. Cut a *weft piece* to match the size and shape of the partial warp. I sketched the weft piece shown here by laying a piece of tracing paper on top of the partial warp and tracing the overall weft shape. Then I cut out the weft shape and cut it into strips.
3. Weave the weft strips into the open edge of the warp slits.

The illustrations below are meant to help you decipher how the warp and weft papers are cut (you'll see them in every project in Chapter 5). You can see curvy partial slits are cut vertically in the warp paper, and the weft piece is cut horizontally into four curvy strips.

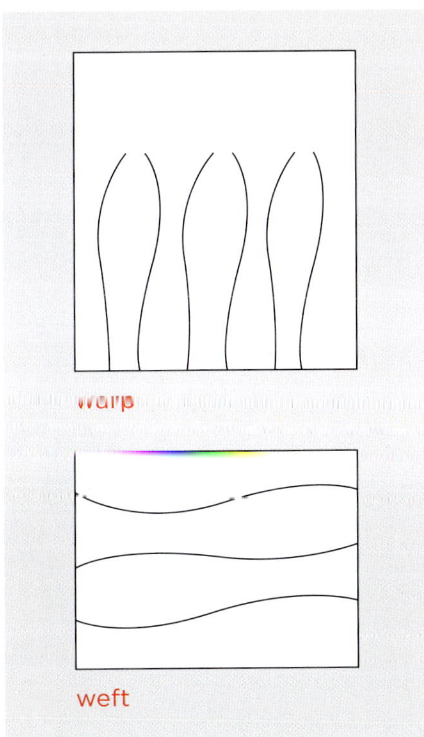

WEAVING ON A PAPER LOOM

A *paper loom* resembles a traditional cloth handloom, and this is the weaving method I use most—the warp is one solid piece with slits, and loose weft strips are woven in.

Making and Using a Paper Loom

1. Begin with two sheets of paper: an 11" × 8½" warp sheet and a 9" × 8½" weft sheet. Measure and draw guidelines 1" from the top and bottom (8½") edges of the warp sheet, if you wish. Draw the guidelines in pencil; you can erase these later.
2. Using a cutting knife, cut vertical slits in the warp sheet between the guidelines, spacing them 1 to 1½" apart. These slits can be straight or curved; they just cannot cross each other.
3. Cut the weft piece into curved strips and keep them in order.
4. Weave the first weft strip into your warp, over/under/over/under. Push it up into place.
5. Weave the next weft strip in the opposite fashion (under/over/under/over).
6. Continue weaving, alternating the weaving pattern as in steps 4 and 5.

WORKING THE LAST STRIP

When you get to the last strip, it may not fit due to take-up. This is especially common when weaving curved strips, since some wide curved parts of a weft strip will have to be woven through skinnier curved slit areas in the warp.

Three Ways to Get the Last Strip In

1. Trim the last strip before weaving it in. Always trim the straight edge, if there is one.
2. If you have extra space on your warp paper, cut each slit a little longer to accommodate the last weft strip.

3. I call this last method "paper gymnastics" because it involves a lot of flipping around.

- Slip one end of the last weft strip into place.
- Flip the opposite end of the strip over, curling it back toward the edge where you started, and slip it through the next warp slit, taking advantage of the extra space above it to slide it into place (A).
- Pull the weft strip all the way through the slit and shimmy it down into place (B).
- Repeat, flipping the warp sheet over as needed to get the final weft strip into the remaining warp slits.

Tips When Weaving Using a Paper Loom

- I think about economy when weaving, so if possible, I usually cut more warp slits and fewer weft strips. Having fewer loose strips to weave in saves time, and more warp slits allows you to accomplish this without sacrificing detail.
- Sometimes I weave from the center of the loom out, especially if I can foresee that this will help the strips fit into the loom better; this is particularly relevant when I'm weaving curved or shaped strips.
- I often flip my entire weaving over and work from the back side, reorienting it as needed.
- A weaving tool can speed up the weaving process and make pulling strips through the warp easier.

How to Use a Weaving Tool

1. Pinch the clamp and grab one end of the weft strip with the weaving tool.
2. Weave the long, flat end of the tool through the warp slits (ahead of your strip).
3. Gently pull the flat end of the tool, sliding the weft strip through the slits.
4. Release the clamp.

CUTTING WINDOWS

Cutting windows into the layers of a weaving adds a visual element by revealing the paper beneath. As you will see on your journey, you can use this technique to create patterns, build shapes into your weavings, or let light shine through the layers. I find the window-cutting process to be meditative.

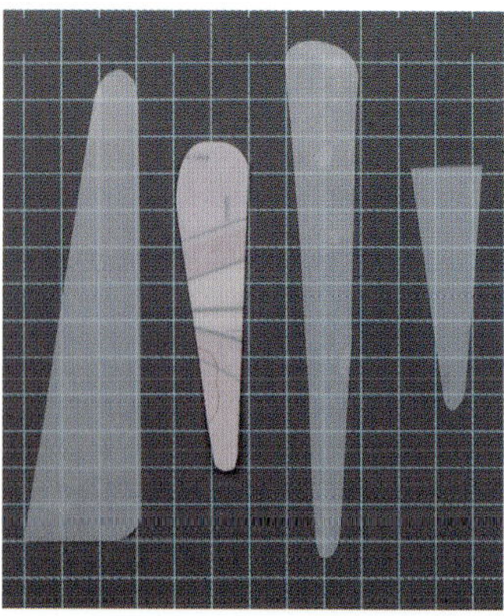

You might want to create a few different sizes of mini cutting mats to slip into skinny and wider openings. Note that the strips will wear out over time.

How to Cut a Window

1. Cut a piece of flexible plastic place mat into a long, tapered strip, approximately 5" long, 1⁄4" at one end, and 11⁄2" at the other end. Round the ends.
2. Slip this mini cutting mat between the layers of a *woven section*. I always slip the skinny end of a mini mat into the wider side of a woven section because that lets it slide in the farthest and fit into the woven section best.
3. Use a craft knife to cut a window through the top layer of the woven section. Follow the shape of the edges of the woven section, and leave the margins (the window "frame") at least 3⁄16" wide. If you try to make the window frame thinner than this, you might end up with a hole (which you can patch; see the facing page). Move the cutting mat as needed so that it is underneath the section you are cutting. I sometimes slip the cutting mat in one side of the woven section, make my cuts on one edge, and then remove the mat and slip it in on the other side as I'm cutting a window.

To cut a window, slide a mini cutting mat between two woven layers. Use a craft knife to cut through the top layer, being sure to keep the cutting mat underneath the section you are cutting.

Window-Cutting Troubleshooting

Patching holes: If you end up with a hole between the woven layers (1), cut a small piece of a matching paper and glue it onto the back of your weaving to cover the hole (2 and 3).

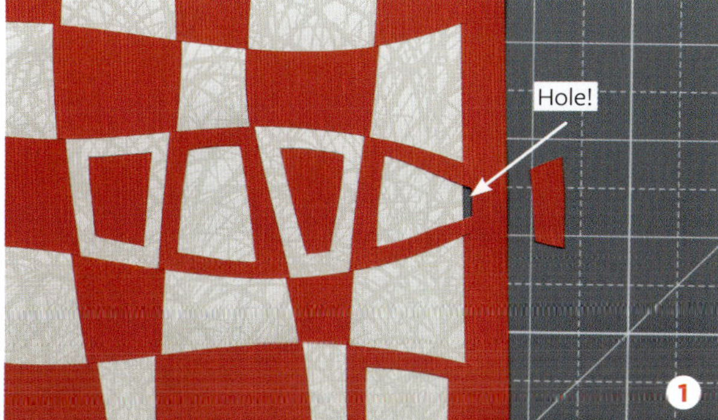

Cut a patch.

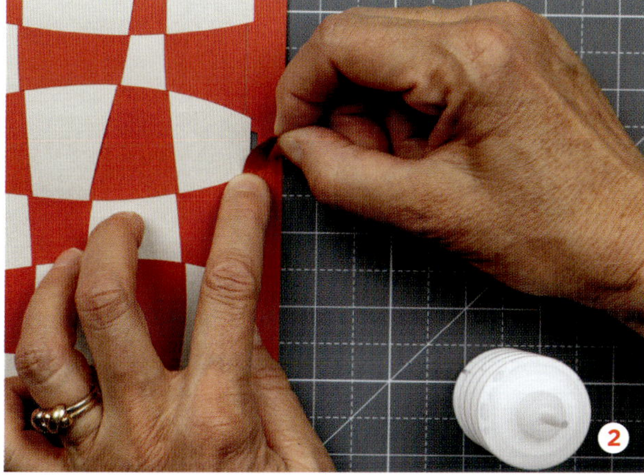

Glue the patch onto the back of the weaving.

The finished patch will be hardly noticeable.

Cutting edge windows: Since the ends of each strip are glued, I usually don't cut windows along the edges of my weavings—it can be tricky to get a mini cutting mat between those glued layers. But sometimes a weaving needs windows on the edges. If you apply just a thin bead of glue (approximately ⅛") to the very edge of each strip, you can still slip your mini cutting mat between the layers of a woven edge section (see below). Once you're experienced, you can also try weaving, cutting windows, and then gluing in that order.

Cut an edge window, then adhere the edge of the strip.

Reasons to Cut Windows

Cutting windows adds potential for illumination, which is how I came up with this process in the first place when I was designing a lamp. This technique can be used to enhance lampshades, lanterns, or weavings displayed to catch natural light.

- Cut windows in one paper on one side of a weaving (see Weaving 24, page 150).
- Cut windows in both papers on one side (see Weaving 25, page 154).
- Cut windows into one paper on both sides (see Weaving 24, top right example, page 153).
- Reveal a shape by cutting windows (see Weaving 24, bottom example, page 153).
- Cut shaped windows or doors (see Weaving 22, page 140).

Developing Your Design Eye

These design principles will undoubtedly come in handy as you progress on your weaving journey. You may wish to start a journal or notebook as you come up with ideas for your own distinctive weaving structures.

Line: One of the beauties of weaving with paper is that your warp and weft strips don't have to be straight! The type of lines you cut can draw the eye differently across the piece. Straight lines evoke order, wavy lines create movement, zigzag lines imply tension, and diagonal lines generate energy.

Amanda Thackray "painted" this artist-made paper with colored pulps to mimic different kinds of floating plants and other debris and simulate the flow of a tidal river, shown here prior to cutting and weaving.

In *River Strata* by Amanda Thackray, the wavy weft lines create a sense of movement—we see rippling water because of the way those lines are cut.

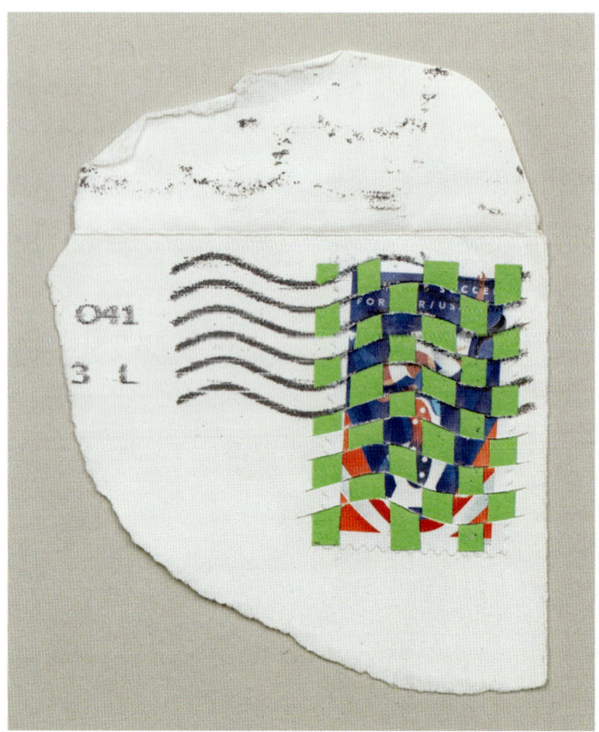

Shape (left): I cut the circular shape in dark green paper, positioned it on the light green paper, and traced the outline of the shape onto the light green paper. Next I cut zigzag horizontal slits in the warp and cut the weft piece into vertical strips. Learn more about weaving shapes in Chapter 5.

Size (right): How tiny can you weave? Notice how I cut the warp slits in this piece along the wavy lines in the postmark.

Shape: Your overall design can be one large shape, or you can weave a shape—cut into strips—into your weaving. Try weaving a triangle or a circle into a square; create an organic shape as your warp and weave into it; cut windows to reveal a shape.

Size: By exploring the size of individual elements, you can achieve very different effects. Scale can help draw attention to certain elements, while creating emphasis and drama. You might try making a tiny weaving (think postage stamp–size) or create a weaving that incorporates different sizes of the same shape.

Space: This is the area around, within, or between images or parts of an image. Positive space is the subject or focal point in your piece; negative space is the area around that positive space. Try these approaches: Weave into the positive space; weave into the negative space; weave one way in the negative space and another way in the positive space.

Typography: Using fonts, lettering, and/or text can add visual interest and artistry to your weaving, even when your text is illegible. Try weaving text with an image or weaving big text with small text.

Space (top left): As an example of weaving into the positive space, I cut lots of windows into this shaped weaving to reveal the positive silhouette shape. It is sometimes helpful to look at the back of a weaving (top right), because it reveals information—the back of this weaving has no windows.

Typography (bottom right): *Going in Circles*, by Lisa Rayne Actor, combines an inkjet print of the artist's original painting with text that relates to the image. For Lisa, the piece represents a crossroads in art making, frustration, and experimentation in combining original art, placed text, and weaving.

Balance: I chose to weave calm wavy lines through the yin-yang symbol to create a sense of balance.

Balance: Think of each element in your weaving as having a certain weight. Balance is achieved when elements are organized to distribute their visual weight in a pleasing way. While asymmetry (imbalance) can be unusual and eye-catching, symmetry (balance) can infuse a sense of calm.

Contrast: Placing different elements next to one another—for example, light next to dark, thick next to thin, or small next to large—can highlight their differences. Explore contrast by varying the widths or colors of weft strips and/or warp pieces, or by weaving thick, light-colored pieces with thin, dark-colored pieces (see the facing page for an example of how small changes in contrast can have a dramatic effect).

Making Subtle Changes in Color, Pattern, and Size

One of the biggest challenges that Weave Through Winter participants and I have is anticipating how two papers will look when woven together. Sometimes they look amazing side by side but, when woven together, don't have enough contrast. This can relate to color, pattern, and weaving structure.

The two works by Cathy Moore pictured below are an excellent example of what happens when you make slight adjustments in contrast.

The piece on the left demonstrates what happens when you don't have enough contrast—the color values are too similar and the patterns in the papers blend together. The end result is an effect that's too busy, making the shape of the house hard to see.

In Cathy's second attempt, she used two plain papers (with no pattern and more contrast), starting with a typical over/under weaving structure and veering from that to highlight the windows. She cut panes into the upper windows and wove in a narrow strip above and below each lower window for more definition. She tucked roses growing on a trellis at the base of the house.

Contrast: Not having enough contrast in warp and weft strips (left) creates an image that's difficult to read. A second attempt at the same project (right), using wider strips with more contrast, is much clearer.

Direction: Adding direction to your weaving structure gives viewers a path to move their eye in a desired pattern or direction. Look at the letters *Z*, *L*, and *S* and how their lines flow—you can create these same directions in your piece. Try including a horizon line to evoke a landscape.

Dominance and emphasis: When you make one element dominant over others, it heightens the level of contrast and can create a focal point in your work. Create one element that dominates the rest of your weaving (think of how a tree can dominate a landscape or a statue can dominate a garden view).

Pattern, repetition, rhythm, and movement: Units that are repeated in an organized way form a pattern. Repetition can help tie individual elements together and generate a rhythm between lines and shapes. Rhythm creates a sense of movement, direction, and flow in a piece, which brings the work to life. In general, weaving itself creates an over/under pattern (think of a checkerboard), but you might also try responding to the pattern in the paper by coming up with a similar or contrasting pattern in your cut lines.

Direction: I wove into the road to draw the viewers eye down the lane. The shape of the weaving, defined by the existing roadway, creates a sense of perspective as well.

Pattern, repetition, rhythm, and movement: Laurie Moorhead chose a weaving structure to convey the importance of weaving in most historical cultures. The warp base is a print of a floral painting, and the weft is a gel monoprint by the artist.

Framing: There are many ways to frame a weaving. One simple solution is to frame your weaving with paper strips, as I have done here.

Framing: Framing can be for looks or for functionality, but either way, it should complement your piece. Frames can also be implied through an element like color. Enhance your weaving by framing it with strips. Highlight part of your weaving by framing it in a contrasting color. Or use heavier or unusual strips to create a border around your weaving.

Harmony, unity, and composition: Every detail in a piece should work with the others. Sometimes adding one element can create unity, at other times, less is more. Weave a unifying element into your piece by incorporating some of the characteristics (e.g., color, texture) of other elements in your weaving.

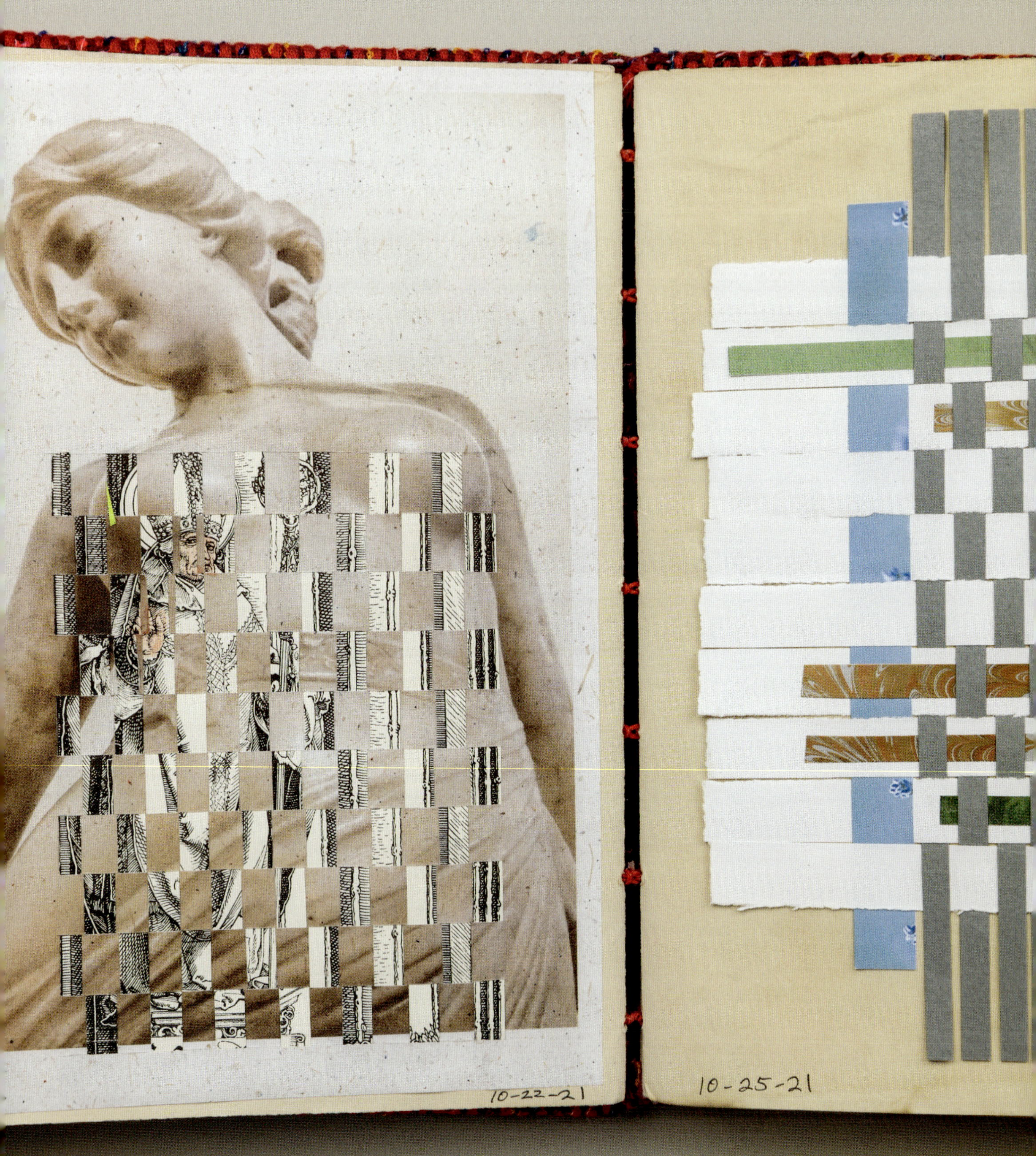
10-22-21
10-25-21

4

ESTABLISHING A DAILY PRACTICE

A daily creative practice is a great way to deepen your relationship to craft and cultivate a routine. In this chapter, I'll share tools and advice for establishing a regular practice that's right for you.

If you really know how to live, what better way to start the day than with a smile? Your smile affirms your awareness and determination to live in peace and joy. How many days slip by in forgetfulness? What are you doing with your life? Look deeply and smile. The source of a true smile is an awakened mind.

—**Thich Nhat Hanh**, Buddhist monk, peace activist, and author of many books including *Present Moment Wonderful Moment*

◂ Detail from a book of paper weavings by Rebecca Winter (see page 67)

Cultivating Flow

I've always admired my husband, who can immerse himself in his writing and tune everything else out. Time and all worldly cares seem to vanish, and he is transported to another world. I know that doesn't happen naturally—he has perfected this skill over time. Just as a runner doesn't put their shoes on for the first time and run a six-minute mile, it takes practice. My own state of flow is different: I always have one eye on the clock and one part of my brain tuned to what I need to accomplish next. When I participate in the daily practice during Weave Through Winter (I do this annually with my class), so many things begin happening due to that daily commitment. I start to anticipate the papers I will weave, how I will respond to the daily prompt, and the shape and structure of my weaving. During those 30 days, weaving enters my psyche, and I start to see things all around me that spark weaving ideas. Sometimes I even dream about weaving.

I tend to think (perhaps overthink!) through each weaving before sitting down to weave, but I can't stress enough how much I get out of the actual weaving process: From touching the paper to moving strips around to weaving/unweaving/reweaving, my brain comes alive in a different way. I look forward to this state of flow—my thoughts, the materials, and the process all work in tandem—and although the weavings are what can be seen and experienced, the ongoing thoughts and overall process are almost more valuable to me than the finished project. I hope you will find and enjoy your own form of flow on your paper weaving journey.

Getting Out of a Creative Slump

Among the benefits of paper weaving is the shift in perspective it offers, which can propel you out of a creative impasse. I received this note from Wendy Rochman of Boulder, Colorado, who was a Weave Through Winter participant as I was working on this manuscript: "Your class has me fired up. I was in a creative slump for two years due to several persistent health crises. Now I'm on my way forward with renewed purpose. Deep gratitude for your encouragement."

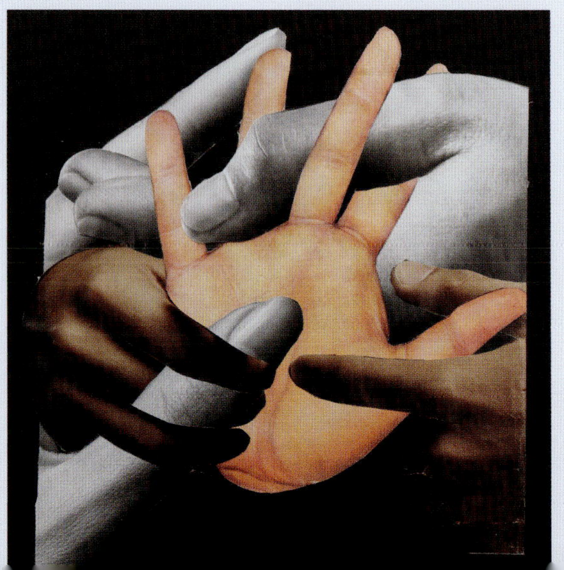

Wendy Rochman cut out images of hands from magazines and wove them together.

12 Benefits of a Daily Practice

1. Developing a new skill (practice makes perfect)
2. Kick-starting your creativity
3. Allocating time to experiment and try new ideas
4. Establishing a routine
5. Developing creative courage
6. Creating momentum
7. Challenging yourself
8. Exploring paper in new ways
9. Sparking inspiration through repetition
10. Engaging in paper weaving as a meditative practice
11. Getting out of a creative funk/overcoming a creative block
12. Focusing on something other than personal woes or current events

A History of Daily Challenges

In the early 2000s, Michael Bierut began challenging his graduate graphic design students at the Yale School of Art to come up with a design project that they could repeat every day for 100 days (the length of a semester). On day 100, each student had 15 minutes to present their project to the class. Student projects ranged widely in content—from taking a picture each day with a stranger to picking a paint chip out of a bag and responding to it with a short essay. I would have loved that class!

Now an annual event on Instagram, #the100DayProject is a free global art project for all kinds of creatives, who are charged with choosing an action, doing it consistently for 100 days, and sharing the process online.

In recent years, 30-day challenges have become popular, including Carve December (rubber stamping), Februllage (collage), Inktober (printmaking), and Popuptober, to name a few.

Whether you are a full-time artist, a part-time crafter, or new to making, I invite you to find your way into creativity on this 30-day paper weaving journey. If weaving daily feels daunting, or if your goal is simply to learn the techniques, feel free to take the journey at a different pace.

The Intermittent Daily Practice

Doing something daily is a commitment, and I have seen so many people give up or never even get started. I think of my own paper weaving journey as an *intermittent* daily practice because—other than brushing my teeth and exercising—I don't have an ongoing daily practice. I do participate in Weave Through Winter every year with my students—for 28 (or 29) days during the month of February. I can sustain this practice, and every year I look forward to getting into the flow!

Here are some helpful tips I've gathered for starting and sticking to a daily practice.

1. **Set goal(s).** Do you want to weave for 30 days in a row, or is your goal to create for an hour a day—or is this journey about mastering paper weaving techniques? Are you looking to jump-start your creativity, gain creative courage, or create a body of work? It is helpful to define your goal(s) so that you can reflect on them throughout your journey (see tip 11, "Reflect").

2. **Establish project parameters.** The clearer you are about the specifics of your project, the simpler it will be to stick to a plan. The paper weaving journey you'll embark on in Chapter 5 already offers two parameters—a structural technique and a prompt—but you might want to set other limits as well.
   - Try making every weaving the same size.
   - Select from your paper stash, rather than purchasing new papers.

3. **Create a routine.** The only way I have found to sustain a daily practice is to work it into my daily life.
   - When will you weave? You might need to try different times to figure out when you feel most creative and what fits best with everything else going on in your life. I like to weave at the beginning of the day when I have the

A Coach's Advice

Cynthia Morris is a coach for writers, artists, and entrepreneurs (and a practitioner of all three disciplines) and founder of Original Impulse and has led many 30-day writing workshops. The purpose of these challenges is not to train her clients to do something every day but rather to help them forge a relationship with writing. The constraints of a daily practice help your inner artist or writer establish a routine, so that creating becomes part of your daily life. Then, when you're working on a project outside of the daily practice, you will be motivated, trained, and ready to show up.

most energy, but others like to do their daily practice at the end of the day as a way of winding down. Be flexible, because your weaving time may have to change—your kid might get sick, or an appointment or unexpected travel could interfere with your scheduled weaving time.

- Set a time limit. I usually weave for about an hour (which doesn't always include the time I spend thinking about the prompt and coming up with my idea). You might think you need several hours to accomplish a weaving, but when you finally get around to doing it, it doesn't take that long! Having a time limit can really help you get something done. You might even try setting a timer.

4. **Focus on process over product.** Let's be honest: You are not supposed to create 30 masterpieces in 30 days. The process of the daily practice can be more fulfilling than each individual weaving. Enjoy the process!

Silhouettes as Parameters

Gina Pisello has taken my Weave Through Winter course multiple times, and she often sets her own parameters. In 2023 she created a series of silhouettes, inspired by the vintage paper silhouettes in her collection. *Quarterdeck* incorporates a vintage file folder, silhouette paper, gold origami paper, black lokta paper, numbers and letters typed on a vintage Underwood portable typewriter, and rubber-stamped letters and numbers. The set of cards references recurring dreams.

5. **Get out of your head—let your hands do the work!** I am guilty of trying to think through every step in my process before I even start weaving. There are definite advantages to planning, but I encourage you to experiment with your daily practice from time to time. There can be something incredibly freeing in simply cutting strips and moving them around on your worktable.

6. **Create a dedicated workspace.** If you must clear off the dining room table and set up your supplies in order to weave (and then clean up after weaving), you are less likely to stick to a daily practice.
   - If you can't dedicate a space to weaving, try keeping your materials on a tray or in a box that you can tuck away when you aren't working.
   - Beverly Frey, a regular Weave Through Winter participant, tapes a paper grocery bag to the edge of her worktable, and a simple swipe across her tabletop removes her weaving scraps so she can start fresh the next day.

7. **Create community and accountability.** Making art can be lonely and isolating, so finding or creating community can certainly help. It is inspiring to see what others are creating; it is a challenge (in a good way) to keep up with a friend or a group; and it can be motivating to share your work with others. In my Weave Through Winter online class, participants share a photo of their weaving each day, often accompanied by a comment.

Workspace: Taping a paper bag to the edge of your worktable will make clearing it off easy! Simply swipe your paper scraps off the table and into the bag. I like to keep any leftover strips and make them into strip weavings.

Small Daily Steps Lead to Big Things over Time

Collage artist Janice McDonald received a page-a-day diary as a gift in 2019, but since she already had a planner for the year, she didn't use it. That is, until later in the year, when she saw it on her desk, along with some paper scraps, and had an aha moment. Janice began creating a collage a day in the tiny 3" × 5" datebook, using leftover paper pieces from her commission work. This small-scale setup with minimal equipment fits her lifestyle—everything goes in a little pouch, and she even brings this diary on trips so she can engage with her daily practice wherever she is. She continues to create these collages as a meditation at the end of each day (2024 marked six years).

Janice posts daily on Instagram. Her followers hold her accountable—if she misses a day, they check on her. She has gained attention from these posts, which has led to collaborations with other artists, invitations to speak about her work, and a feature in the *London Times* ("Could You Create One New Thing Every Day? Meet the Artists Who Do").

For Janice, it isn't the daily collages that are the most important thing. Some collages are good, and some are failures. It is the *process* of creating daily that keeps her going and stimulates ideas for other projects. And the overall project—a chunky book filled with 365 collages—is what holds value.

"It really helps me see how to simplify and has made me more confident in my approach to my overall practice," Janice observes. "The daily collages are exploratory and don't need to be precise, and certain things come out of that. For example, I might discover a new way of looking at color, or I might see a new juxtaposition for shapes. The daily practice makes me look at things differently and informs my larger collage practice."

In response to a call (from *Cut Me Up* magazine) for collage works about environment, Janice McDonald decided to consider landscape from an aerial perspective. Weaving seemed like a way to both reference and obscure elements related to our gridded-off land use. She cut straight lines to create a warp. The horizontal papers were ripped against a ruler to soften the edges a bit.

Here are some suggestions for building community and keeping yourself accountable:

- Make a commitment to yourself by keeping a journal.
- Put your weaving dates on a calendar or a checklist.
- Try the paper weaving journey (see Chapter 5) with a friend or creative partner or find an accountability buddy who can help keep you on track (and vice versa). This could be as simple as texting "I did my weaving today" or as elaborate as sharing a photo of your weaving and talking about your experience. Keep it simple.
- Some of us don't need accountability, but partnerships can still be powerful. Seek out peers or groups that provide you with motivation, inspiration, and a place to share, critique, and learn. I have a weekly meeting with an accountability buddy, and, often, just telling her something out loud helps me get it done!

8. **Let go of perfection.** Creating a daily practice allows you to focus on process over product and progress over perfection. Doesn't *weave daily* sound easier than *produce 30 paper weavings*? There is a lot of research about visualizing the process (any process) one step at a time, rather than visualizing an outcome, such as winning the race or getting an A. Perfection can get in the way of getting started: You don't have the right tools; you need to order the perfect papers; you don't have time . . . Just START.

9. **Share far and wide.** Tell your family and friends about your project, or choose to engage coworkers, business associates, or a wider network online. My hunch is that interest will grow over time—people who are following you will begin to anticipate what you're doing each day, especially if you write about it and share images. And sharing your project will elicit responses you cannot foresee. I find joy in simply sharing what I am thinking about each day as I weave—sometimes that relates to the weaving process, and other times it has more to do with things that are going on in my daily life. You might be surprised about the impact you are making on others. They are waiting to see what you do!

   - Post on IG and tag your weavings #APaperWeavingJourney. Search this hashtag to find weavings by others who have taken this journey.
   - I shared my weavings on my blog in 2013, and a childhood friend purchased 10 in the series to give to her family as holiday gifts. She had such fun choosing the weavings, finding frames, gifting them to her family, and telling them about my weaving project.

Rebecca Winter's artist's book houses 87 paper weavings.

10. **Document and organize.** This is an extra step, but it can be exceptionally worthwhile.

- Store your weavings in a box or album as you make them (see the album project on page 178).
- Take process photos. Sometimes, when you cut two papers up and weave them back together, it is hard to remember how you got there. It can be fun to see where you started and how you proceeded along the way. Maybe there are steps you will want to re-create in a future weaving. And don't forget to snap a photo of your finished weaving.
- Keep a journal. Document how you responded to a prompt, the papers you used, and the process. I find that once I begin weaving, I stop thinking, because the actual process is mindless, even meditative. I tend to forget what I was thinking about when I'm done, because it is time to start the next weaving. Don't forget to jot down ideas for future weavings!
- Keep a sketchbook.
- Hang your weavings on a wall so that you can see your progress.
- Sign and date each weaving.

11. **Reflect.** You can reflect at any point on your journey, especially if you get stuck. Give yourself some grace and make adjustments as needed.

- Are you fulfilling your goal(s) from tip 1?
- How does the practice fit into your other daily commitments?
- Do you feel lighter, happier, more whole?

5 YOUR PAPER WEAVING JOURNEY

Your paper weaving journey begins with a few simple weavings that will reinforce the basic skills you learned in Chapter 2. As you work your way through these 30 projects, you will acquire more complex techniques, and I hope you will end up inventing some of your own.

The constraints of a daily practice help your inner artist or writer establish a routine, so that creating becomes part of your daily life. Then, when you're working on a project outside of the daily practice, you will be motivated, trained, and ready to show up.

—**Cynthia Morris**, coach for writers, artists, and entrepreneurs and founder of Original Impulse

Things to Consider as You Embark on Your Journey

Paper size and type: For context, I list the sizes of the papers I used, but there are no limits. I also share the types of papers I chose, for inspirational purposes, but, of course, you can choose your own.

Warp and weft thumbnails: These accompany each weaving project and are meant to give you a quick visual cue to how the warp and weft papers are cut.

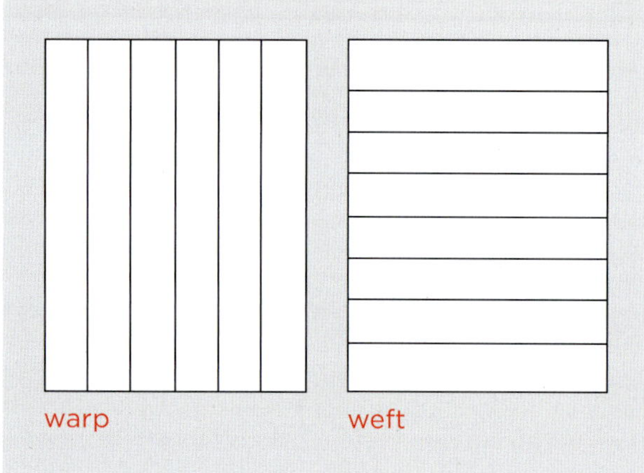

This warp and weft thumbnail indicates that the warp is cut into 6 uniform vertical strips and the weft is cut into 8 uniform horizontal strips.

Prompts: Each project is accompanied by a prompt, which is meant to help you generate ideas for your weavings. Every prompt is open to interpretation, and you're encouraged to come up with your own creative twist.

In my online class, some participants love the prompts, others use them occasionally, and some shy away from them altogether. This is your journey. If you find them helpful, please use them. I've created a printable list of prompts (follow the link under Prompts and Templates on page 210). I like to hang my prompt list in a place where I see it frequently—I often look at it a day ahead, so that I can start brainstorming. You can also jot down weaving ideas right on the prompt list, based on the prompts as they come to you. Feel free to make up your own prompts, too.

Artists' variations: For each of the 30 projects, you will see two examples, created by Weave Through Winter class participants, featuring unique approaches to the prompts and techniques.

Technique: Each project features a structural technique, designed to guide you through the process of mastering a series of simple to advanced paper weavings.

Getting Started

Before beginning your journey, consider putting your things in order:

- Organize your paper.
- Set up your workspace.
- Create folders (physical or digital ones) to document your progress as you go.
- Start a journal (for notes, ideas, and sketches).
- Decide where you will store your weavings (on the wall, in a box, in a notebook in plastic sleeves).

Weaving Prompts

The prompts in each of the following 30 projects can serve as a jumping-off point of inspiration. Each is open to interpretation—use them to generate ideas and come up with your own creative twist!

1: Recycle

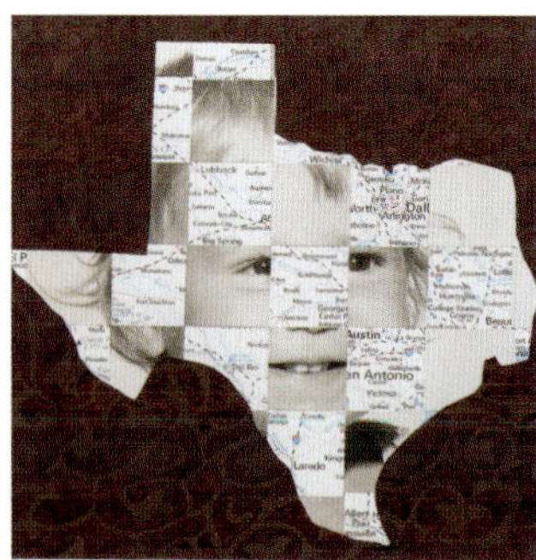

2: Roots

3: Joy

4: World

5: Nature

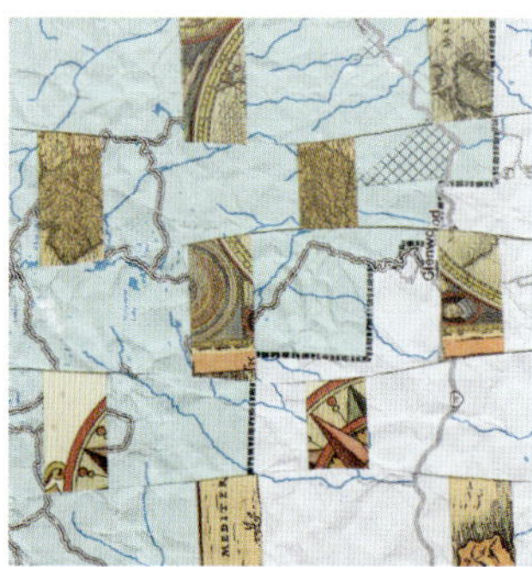

6: Travel

7: Landscape

8: Random

9: Contrast

10: Perspective

11: Routine

12: Window

13: Direction

14: Circle

15: Concentric

16: Ephemera

17: Silhouette

18: Highlight

19: Symbol

20: Winding

21: Crossing

22: Treasure

23: Waves

24: Light

25: Layer

26: Variety

27: Modular

28: Breathe

29: Angle

30: Puzzle

Weaving 1

Prompt: Recycle

Straight to the Point

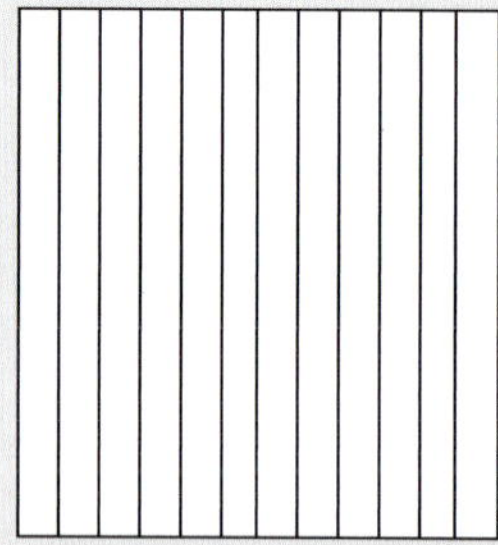

warp

weft

Technique

Vary the width of the warp and weft strips.

Materials

- Warp paper: 7" × 6¼" sheet music, cut into ½" strips
- Weft paper: 7" × 6¼" wallpaper remnant, cut into 1" strips

Let's begin with a straightforward weaving with materials you have on hand. Every day, we're barraged with papers and images, from junk mail to magazines, paper bags, and bill inserts. This project challenges you to weave with what you have. Is there a stack of postcards or magazines piled up in a cabinet or a corner—something you'd usually discard? Try using that for your weaving. Perhaps you can weave in something that has meaning to you, like a copy of a letter, an old family document, or a handwritten recipe. Sometimes what you're looking for is right under your nose.

Instructions

1. Weave the warp and weft strips together using a plain weave.
2. Glue ends and trim, if necessary.

Artists' Variations on the Prompt

Cathy Moore wove together two chocolate bar wrappers, varying the strip widths slightly and cutting some on the diagonal.

Judy Jacques wove together two flour bags. Try weaving two of the same image together to see how they match up.

Weaving 2

Prompt: Roots

Home Sweet Home

Where are your roots? What makes you feel grounded? Your answers might relate to your family, your community, or your sense of purpose. Does a flag, map, written language, or image remind you of your roots? Tap into that feeling and choose materials for this weaving that bring you home. I wove a baby picture with a map of the state I grew up in. Alternatively, you might take a more literal route and weave something related to plant roots.

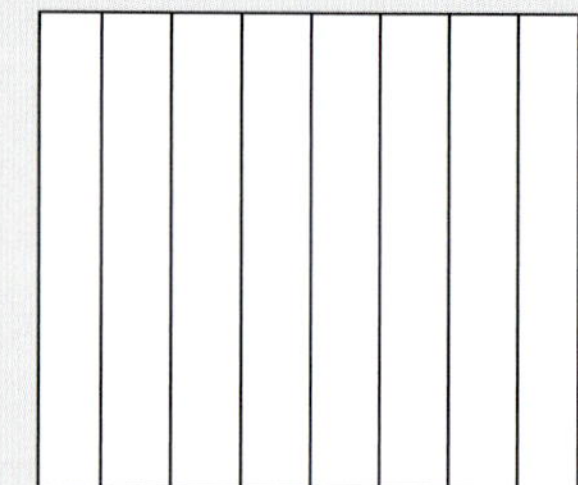

warp

weft

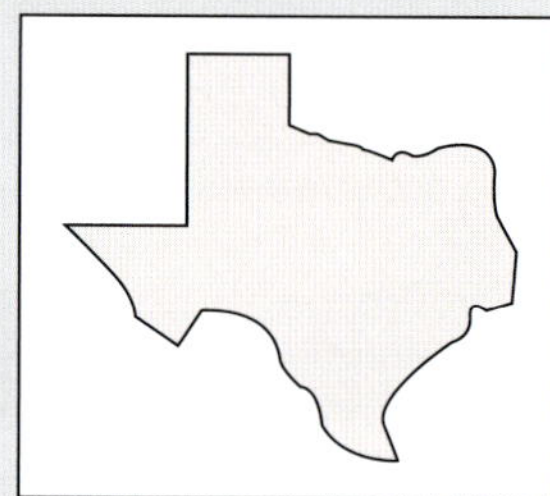

frame

Technique

Weave an odd number of warp strips into an even number of weft strips, or vice versa.

Materials

- Warp paper: Eight 1" strips, cut from a 7" × 8" map of Texas
- Weft paper: Seven 1" strips, cut from a 7" × 8" printed digital image of the author as a baby
- Frame paper (optional): Decorative paper, cut to 7" × 8" with a cutout of the shape of Texas. After weaving, I decided to trim my weaving to make it square.

Instructions

1. Weave the strips together using a plain weave.
2. Glue ends and trim, if necessary, or add a frame, if desired.

Tip

- When weaving a face, strive to leave the eyes visible or else the face will look a bit creepy.

Artists' Variations on the Prompt

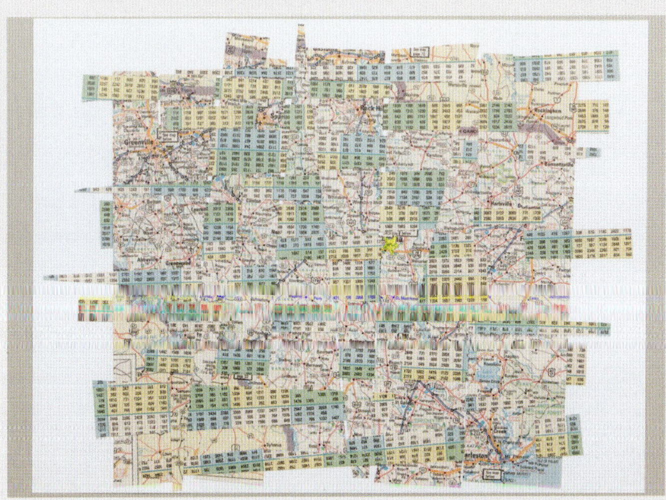

▲ Terry Englehart was rootless growing up because her dad was in the army and her family moved every couple of years. This weaving uses South Carolina road atlas pages and a mileage chart with a gold star near the center marking Fort Jackson, where they lived when Terry was in sixth grade (see the next page for a more detailed view).

◀ Using Japanese shibori origami paper and a Nature Conservancy calendar page, Cathleen Higgins wove an even number of horizontal weft strips (eight) into an odd number of warp strips (seven). Note how the finished weaving has the same papers on top on the left and right sides and alternating papers appear on top and bottom edges.

Fountain Inn
West Pelzer
Kinards

825	1243	197	1430	560	1709	588	623

1184	1277	1794
693	982	1118
543	1070	649

ANDERSON
Belton
Princeton
Court
Wattsville
Laurens
El. 600 ft.
Newberry Coll.
Helena
Clinton
LAURENS
Joanna
Mountville
Waterloo
Cross Hill
L. Greenwood
Coronaco
Greenwood S.P.
Gluck
Honea Path
Erskine Coll.
Donalds
Ware Shoals
Shoals Junction
Starr
Due West
Iva
Antreville
Secession Lake
Cokesbury
Hodges
ABBEVILLE
Lowndesville
Abbeville
El. 597 ft.
Lander Coll.
Greenwood
El. 665 ft.

2313	2308
1101	1479
604	759
1206	1154
1446	1582
2144	2028
743	501
1467	1840
434	609

Greenwood Airport
Ninety Six
Dyson
Chappells
Ninety Six Nat'l. Hist.
Epworth
Batesburg
Ridge Spring
Ward

2701	1480	3001	962	1337	1561	1043
2583	1452	2855	937	1315	1649	931
		174	209	910	55	

1675	319	670	1641
1651	382	727	1601
532	900	672	683
	1335	1039	69

Mount Carmel
Willington
Hickory Knob S.R.
Bobby Brown S.P.
McCORMICK
Eureka
Johnston
Edgefield
EDGEFIELD
Trenton
Colliers
Elijah S.P.
Lincolnton
Clarks Hill L.
Clark Hill Dam
Modoc
New Ellenton
Vaucluse
Graniteville
Par Pond
Snell
BARN

2269	1442	1566	1656
1911	197	1191	673
2901	1490	2078	1756
3082	1911	2289	2151

SAVANNAH RIVER PLANT (U.S. Govt.)

396	1836	256
419	1438	691	1618
1287	583	1387	1103
336	1666	127	2090

Gracewood
page 22
Grovetown
Jackson
Campania

283	414	563	578

1858	701	414	860	1033

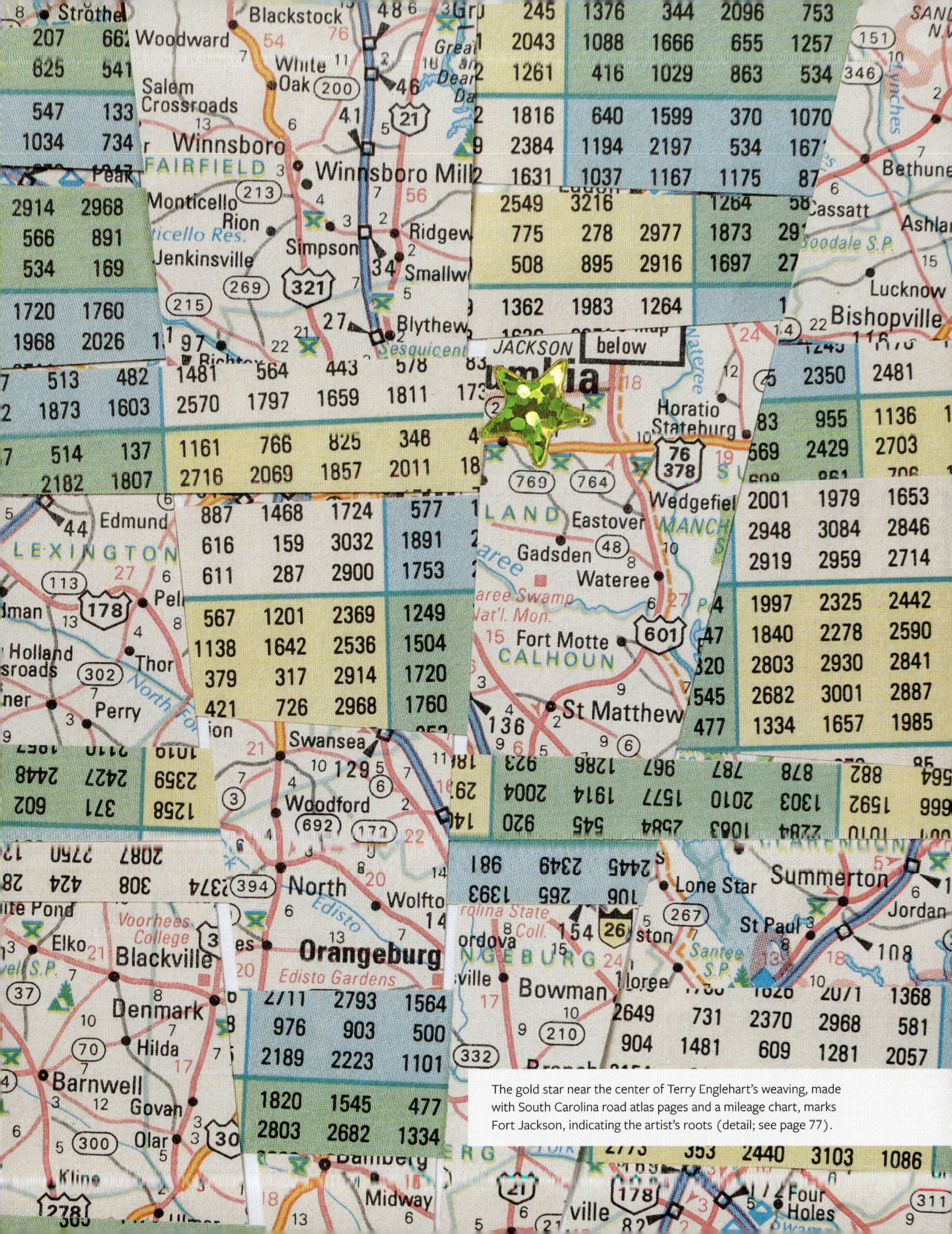

The gold star near the center of Terry Englehart's weaving, made with South Carolina road atlas pages and a mileage chart, marks Fort Jackson, indicating the artist's roots (detail; see page 77).

Weaving 3

Prompt: Joy

Explore the Edge

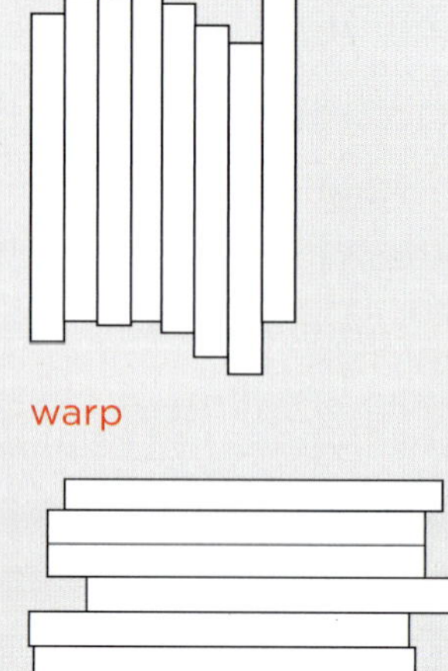

weft

Technique

Stagger your strips or use different lengths to create interesting edges.

Materials

- Warp + weft papers: Fifteen ½" strips cut from 6" squares of Tant origami paper in different colors

What color or pattern brings you joy? This project is all about being joyful in your creation, while also staggering your strips. Use papers that sing to your soul!

Instructions

This approach to strip weaving locks the central strips in place first. Subsequent strips are woven in around the central strips.

1. Interlock the center of four strips, as shown.
2. Add one strip at a time, working your way around the center, following a plain weaving structure. Stagger the ends, if desired.
3. Glue strategically around the outermost connection points until your weaving is stable.

Artists' Variations on the Prompt

▲ I explored the boundaries of one edge while weaving a garden overtaking a city.

◄ Carol Ann Waugh used artist-made paper and black strips to highlight the edges of her weaving.

Weaving 4

Prompt: World

Global Vision

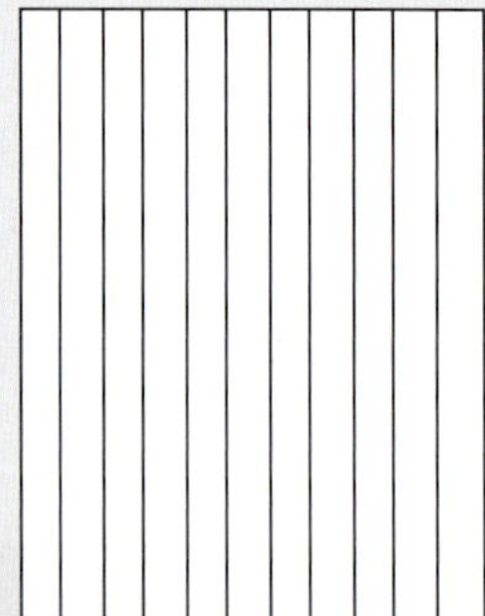

warp

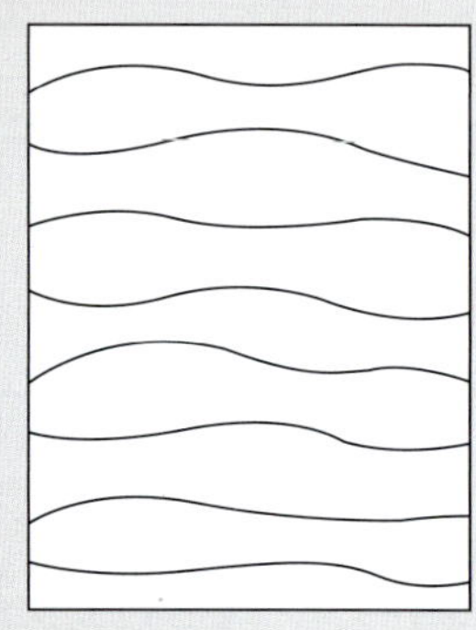

weft

Technique

Weave curved weft strips into straight warp strips.

Materials

- Warp paper: 11" × 8½" travel photo of Crans-Montana, Switzerland, by the author, printed on standard copier paper
- Weft paper: 11" × 8½" travel photo of Lech Zürs, Austria, by the author, printed on standard copier paper

For this weaving, think big—look outside yourself for a theme and think outside the box for your materials. Consider weaving images of a place in the world or of foreign food or languages; newspaper or magazine headlines or articles; or papers that reflect an overall thought about peace in the world.

Instructions

1. Cut the warp paper into straight strips (using the ruler as a guide) and the weft paper into curved strips (or vice versa).
2. Weave, glue ends, and trim, if necessary.

Two starting images

Artists' Variations on the Prompt

Carol Ann Waugh used book pages from a world atlas, toothpicks, and flags. She wove two different maps of the same location and then tucked flags on toothpicks into woven sections to add a three-dimensional element.

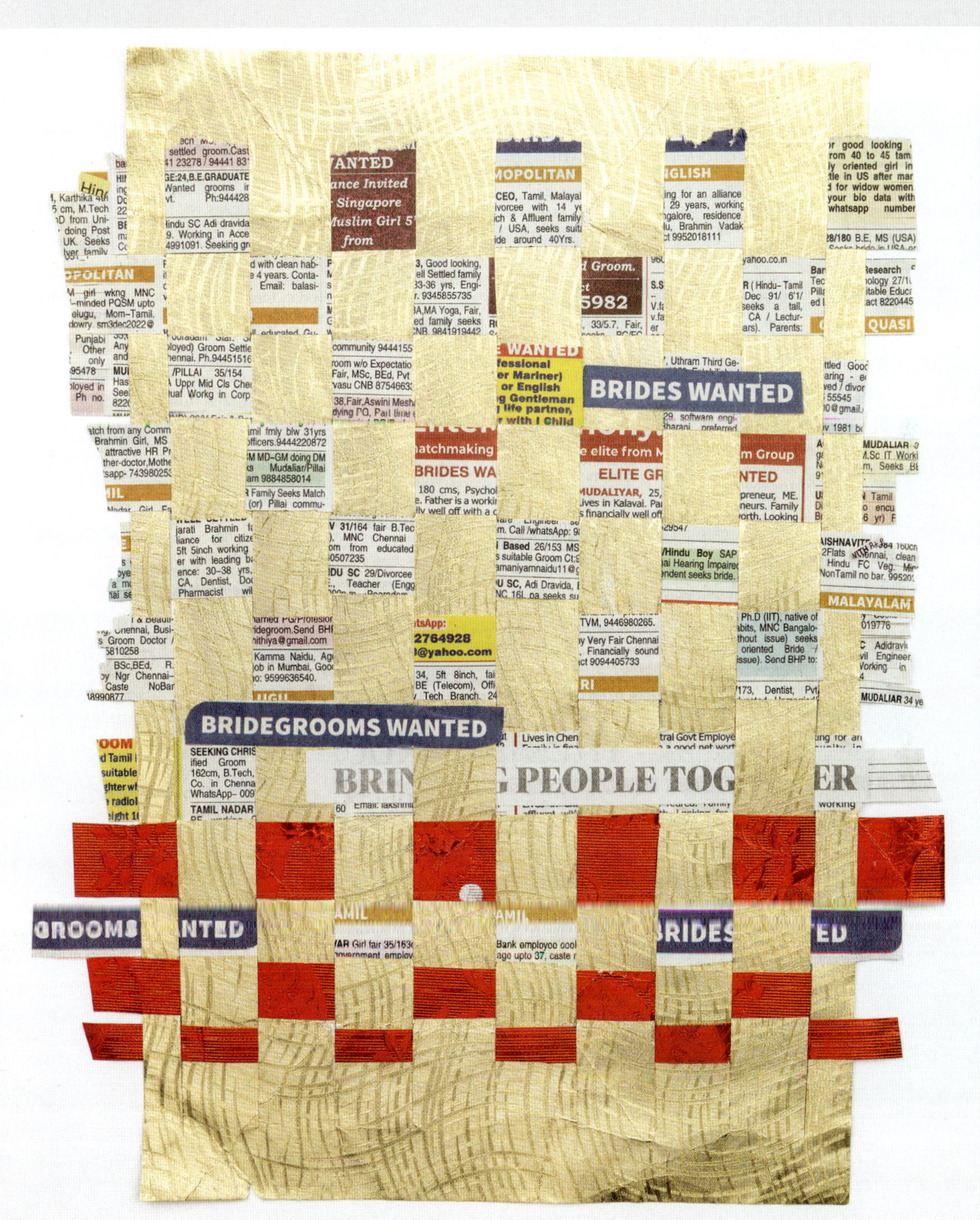

Indira Govindan wove gold wrapping paper (Indian weddings shimmer with gold and glitter) with an Indian newspaper's matrimonial classified ads page, recalling her arranged marriage and how her parents found her husband.

Weaving 5

Prompt: Nature

The Great Outdoors

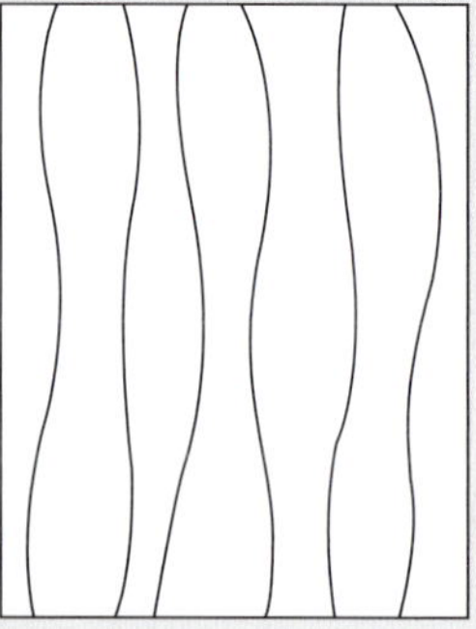
warp

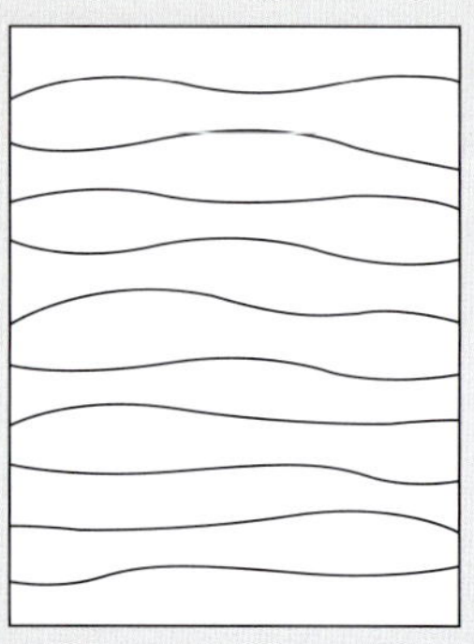
weft

Technique

Weave curved warp strips into curved weft strips.

Materials

- Warp paper: 12" × 8½" marbled jute paper
- Weft paper: 12" × 8½" abaca paper

Nature has inspired artists for centuries. Whether it's the calm of the ocean, the density of the forest, the richness of the earth, or the beauty of the wildlife, colors, textures, and patterns can evoke feelings that connect us with nature. The elements—earth, wind, fire, water—may be a great place to start. Grow something organic with this weaving.

Instructions

1. Cut the warp and weft papers into curved strips (one set horizontal, the other set vertical).
2. Weave, glue ends, and trim, if necessary.

Tip:

There is no need for a ruler or measuring, but when you weave curved strips back together they fit together like a puzzle!

Artists' Variations on the Prompt

▲ In this exercise Kristi Galbraith merged two reproduction Japanese prints into one. She cut a curved warp and a curved weft, then layered and pulled some sections to the front to highlight Mount Fuji and the people, trees, flowers, and water.

► Davida Feder scanned a magazine page, inverted the colors in Photoshop (using the inverse function), and printed both versions on copier paper. This is another example of weaving two of the same image together.

Weaving 6

Prompt: Travel

Dream Vacation

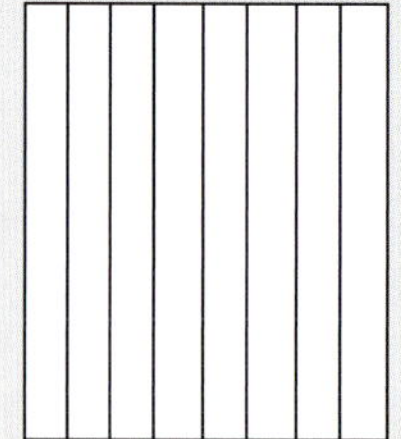

warp

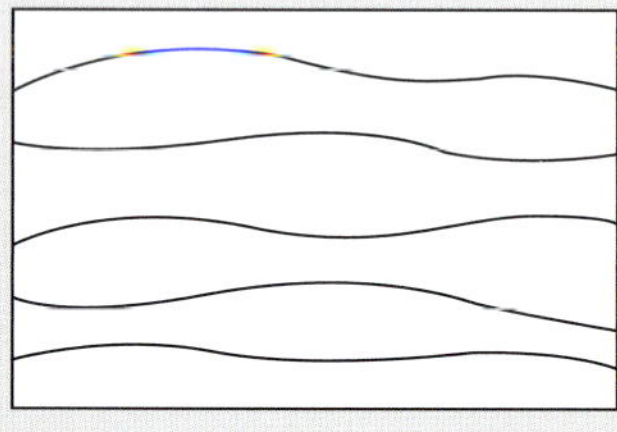

weft

Technique

Add dimension to your strips: Crumple, twist, or fold the strips before weaving. Consider using unusual materials and adding space between the strips as you weave.

Materials

- Warp paper: 5¼" × 4" reproduction map
- Weft paper: 5½" × 7¾" crumpled topographic map of Colorado

Note:
I crumpled the weft piece into a tight ball and then flattened it prior to cutting it into strips, to give it a textured, topographic feel.

Does adventure entice you? Do the sights and sounds of a foreign city or an exotic destination call to you? Have you attended a memorable event? Or is there a museum you've always wanted to visit? Find images or papers that represent your dream travel destination, whether it's in your past or on your bucket list. Use airline stubs, an itinerary, a map, a brochure, or photocopies of printed souvenirs. Let this weaving transport you to a favorite place.

Instructions

1. Cut the papers into strip widths and styles (straight, curvy) of your choice.
2. Weave the warp and weft strips together, leaving space between strips.
3. Glue ends and trim.

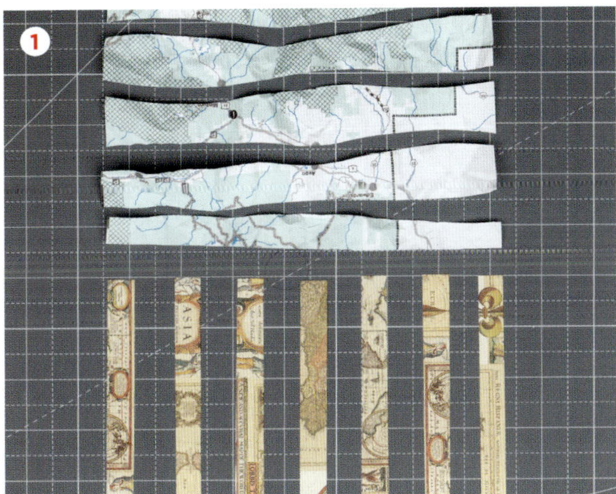

Artists' Variations on the Prompt

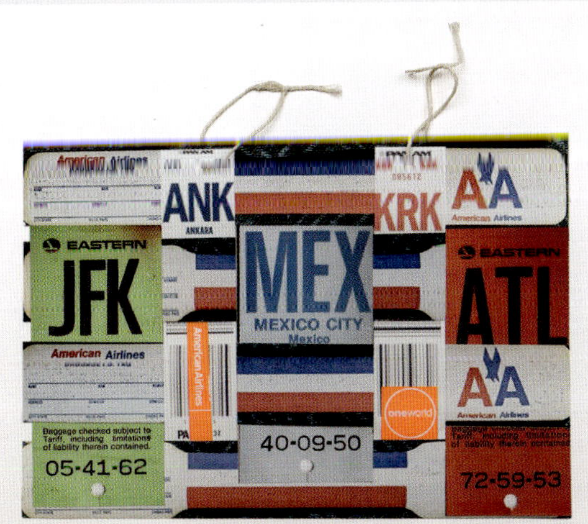

Denise Marshall had just come back from a vacation when she took Weave Through Winter and encountered the prompt "Travel + Unusual Materials." She incorporated her luggage tags and also printed out vintage tags from the internet to weave into the piece.

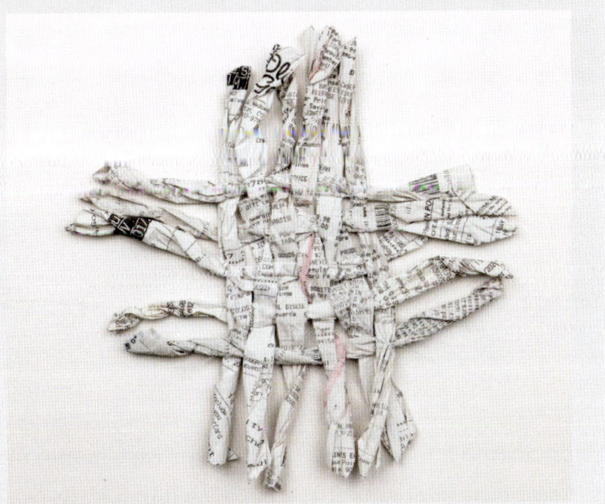

Diane K. Bauerle folded and twisted her receipts from a trip to the grocery store (what a unique response to travel!) and then wove them together, securing them with white sewing thread.

Weaving 7

Prompt: Landscape

What a View!

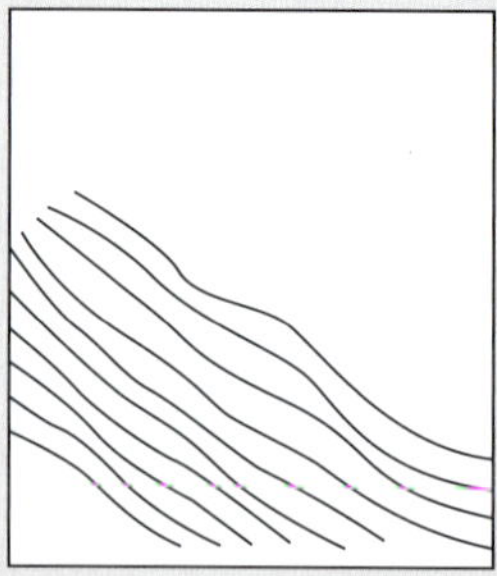

warp

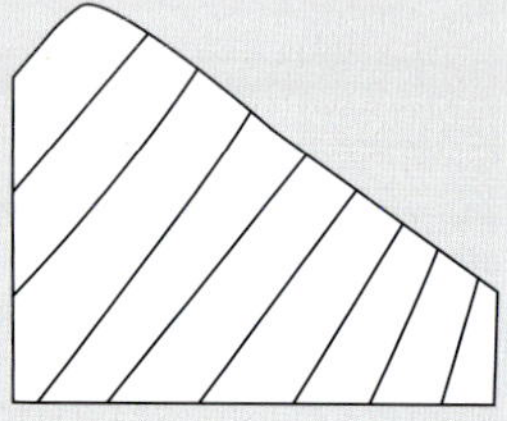

weft

Technique

Weave into part of the warp.

Materials

- Warp paper: 12" × 8½" artist-made cloud paper
- Weft paper: 8½" × 6½" cork paper from Portugal

Note:

I left the top edge of the mountain (weft) strips on top of the weaving, instead of weaving them under, to define the mountain shape.

Many people find that looking out over vast spaces like mountains or oceans is therapeutic. Perhaps that's because it makes us realize that we're all part of something larger than ourselves. Landscapes can be urban (cityscapes), country (forests or fields), tropical (shorelines), or any view that pleases you. Feel free to be a little cryptic or abstract—you don't always have to aim for representational art.

Instructions

Try this simple approach to weaving into a warp by weaving a solid shape that is cut into weft strips. This is a nice segue into full warp weaving.

1. Draw a solid mountain shape in the weft paper (use a photo or clip art as a guide, if you need to). Then cut it out.
2. Place the mountain shape (in reverse) on the back of the warp paper and trace the outline.
3. Cut slits into the warp.
4. Cut the weft piece into strips approximately 1" wide.
5. Weave, glue ends, and trim, if necessary.

Artists' Variations on the Prompt

▲ I cut a solid weft piece and wove it into the slits in the warp paper.

◄ Robin Kessler chose a light cardstock in four colors representing irises because they remind her of the landscapes of her childhood. If you look closely, you can see that the partial weft is connected on the left side, so she slipped the pieces in from the right. She also did some *over-weaving* to add more floral elements.

Weaving 8

Prompt: Random

Simply by Chance

For this weaving, take a break from decision-making and leave your choice up to chance. Randomly pick two strips of paper from your scrap box (ideally, don't even look when you select your papers) and place them on your worktable. Try to forget about how you used the papers previously. Just find a new way to weave these two strips together. If an idea doesn't come to you right away, leave them sitting on your table within view, moving them around on occasion, and be ready to jump in whenever inspiration strikes.

Tip:
A weaving tool comes in handy on this weaving. Pre-thread the weaving tool into the warp slits, attach the strip to the pinch mechanism, and pull it through the warp slits. Voilà! Your strip is woven.

Challenge: Can you think of another way to create a one-strip weaving?

warp

weft

Technique

Weave two strips—just two! This two-strip weaving has a one-strip warp that holds everything together and a one-strip weft, but there are many ways to approach this challenge.

Materials

- Warp paper: 8½" × 2⅛" embossed momigami
- Weft paper: 12" × ½" chiyogami paper
- Special tool: Weaving tool (see Resources, page 210)

Instructions

This is how I wove my strips together, but feel free to come up with your own solution. There is no right answer!

1. Draw vertical guidelines marking where the thin weft strip will be woven into the wider warp strip.
2. Cut random slits into the warp. Cut just beyond the guidelines you drew to give yourself a little extra space for fitting the strip in.
3. Weave, glue ends, and trim, if necessary.

Artists' Variations on the Prompt

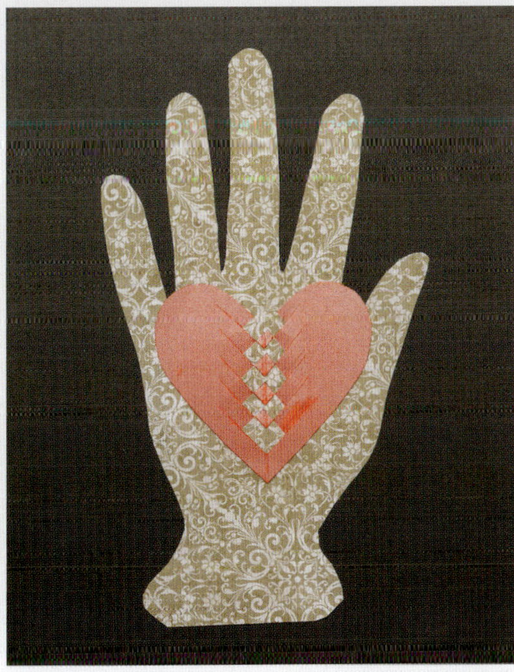

► Kirilka Stavreva chose to evoke Sacred Heart Catholic imagery through the heart-in-hand design, popular in Dutch-German and Scandinavian folk art (see another example on page 23). This secular version of the traditional weaving design was made in response to a prompt for a two-strip weaving and takes the idea of a strip in a new direction.

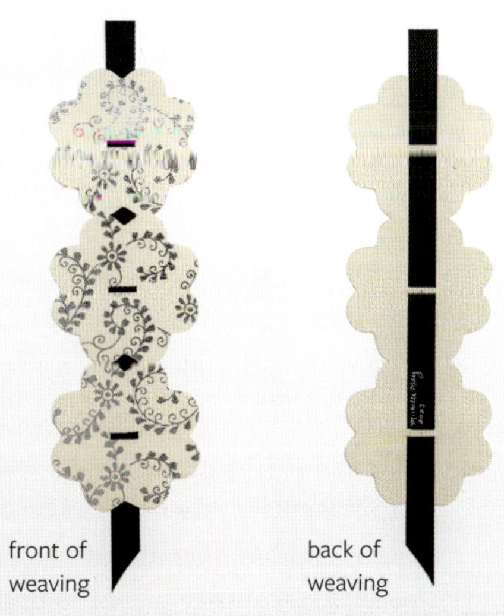

▲ Michelle May cut a flowery strip with unique slits and two diamond-shaped windows to enhance the black paper strip she wove into it.

Weaving 9

Prompt: Contrast

Worlds Collide, in a Good Way

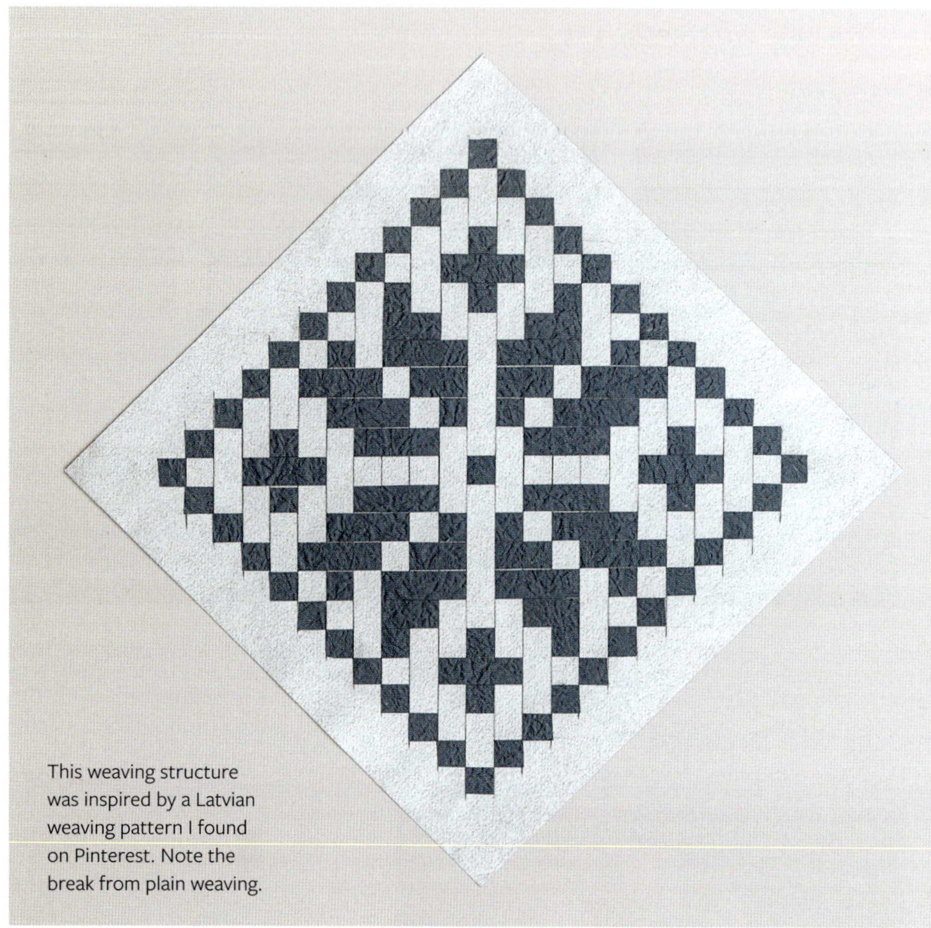

This weaving structure was inspired by a Latvian weaving pattern I found on Pinterest. Note the break from plain weaving.

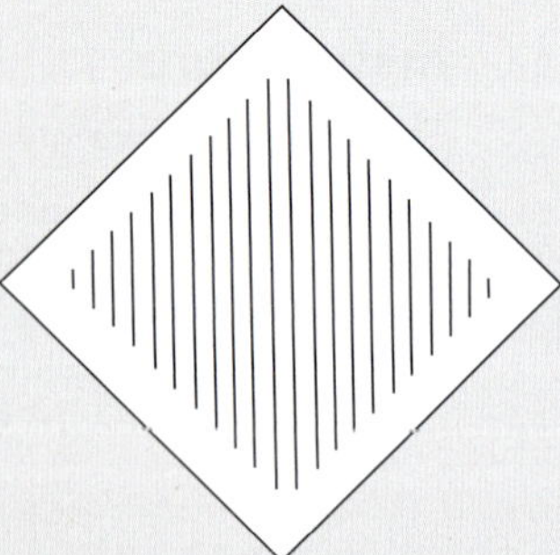

warp

weft

Technique

Weave into a paper loom. This weaving features a solid warp (silver paper) and blue weft strips.

Materials

- Warp paper: 6½" square of silver paper
- Weft paper: 7¼" square of marine blue embossed momigami
- Printed downloadable templates (see link on page 210)
- Special tool: Weaving tool (see Resources, page 210)

Creating contrast in art can lead to unexpected and fascinating results. Placing contrasting elements next to each other invites us to recognize the unique qualities in each of them. Consider pairs of contrasting elements: dark and light, summer and winter, work and play, day and night, city and country. Choose a pair that resonates with you and think of an image that represents each of those contrasting elements. If you choose summer and winter, for instance, your summer image might be a beach scene and your winter image might be a snowcapped mountain. Or keep it simple and pick two solid colors that contrast with each other.

Instructions

1. Print the templates (printing them directly on the back of your project papers will make the next steps simpler).
2. Tape the warp template on top of the warp paper and cut along each horizontal line through both layers of paper to create the warp slits. Discard this template. (If the templates are printed on the back of your project papers, tape your project papers template-side up and simply cut along the warp/weft lines.)
3. Tape the weft template on top of the weft paper and cut through both layers to create the weft strips, keeping them in order as you cut them.
4. Weave: I started weaving in the center with the longest strips, worked my way up to the top, and then wove from center down. The weaving tool came in handy.
5. Glue ends.

Note: I glued the small squares at the very top and bottom of the weaving because they were too tiny to weave in.

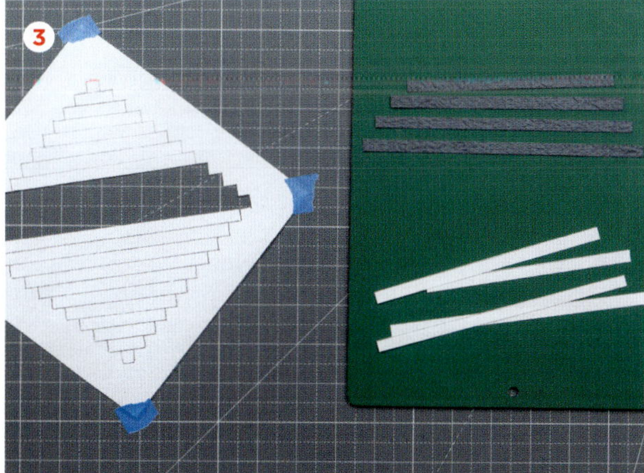

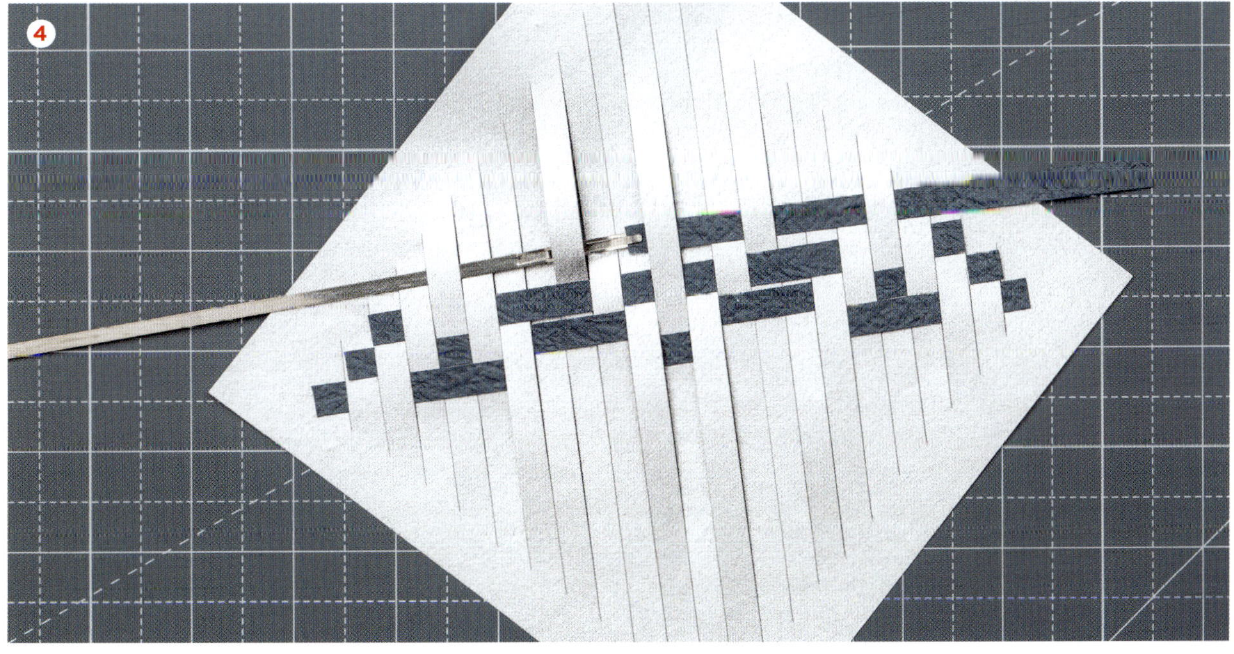

Artists' Variations on the Prompt

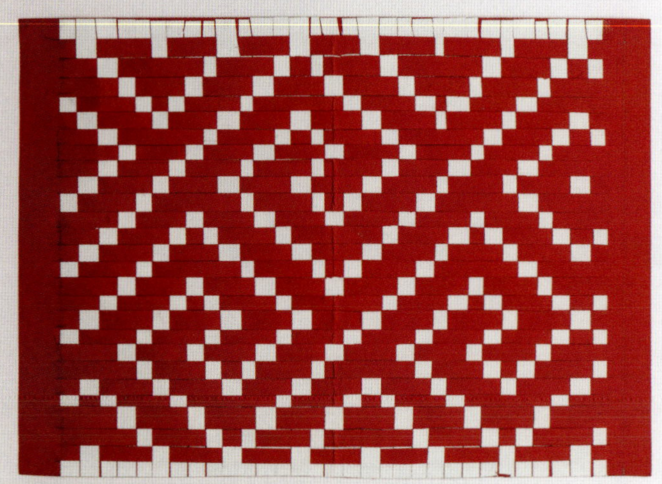

▲ Sarah Morgan was influenced by a weaving structure in the Golden Jubilee edition of *The Paradise of Childhood* (see Suggested Reading, page 211), which includes many historic weaving patterns used in Friedrich Froebel's kindergarten teaching. The open-weave structure reveals its own pattern, while allowing the painting to show through.

◄ Look at the back of this weaving (without the distraction of the painting) to decipher the weaving structure.

A "Magical" Weaving Practice

In 2020, while taking an abstract photography class, a medical problem in Denise Marshall's right arm sometimes prevented her from holding her camera steady. One day, determined to complete her assignment, she took one of her photographs and cut it up vertically. Then she looked at the deconstructed photograph on a white mat board and separated the strips while keeping the image "together." That sparked an idea: Denise took another copy of the same photograph, cut it up horizontally, and numbered the strips to keep them in order. She wove the two images together and liked the results.

Denise says, "I was diagnosed with breast cancer in 2021 and have not stopped weaving: I find it to be a powerful art form that relaxes me and makes me feel whole." I met Denise—online—when she was a participant in my Weave Through Winter online class in 2022. Denise loved the class and found the practice of going to her studio every day to be magical.

She still makes several weavings each week and is in her studio every day. Sometimes she goes to her studio after dinner for a relaxing weave before bed, and she never enters her studio if she is not in a good mood, which is a promise she made to herself when she started this journey.

As a photographer, Denise now sees her images as weavings, so when she goes out to photograph she deliberately selects her subjects. Lately she has been mixing her photographic weavings with the art of encaustic, and she is also making her own marbled paper to incorporate into her weavings.

Denise Marshall created her own weaving structure and wove two photographs she took in Los Angeles—one of the Broad Museum and the other of the Walt Disney Concert Hall. The weaving received an Editor's Choice Award from *Frames* magazine.

Weaving 10

Prompt: Perspective

Fading Away

Perspective, in this case, refers to how something seems to disappear in the distance. A long road goes on until it vanishes into the scenery. A ship gets smaller and smaller as it sails away on the ocean. If you're standing across from an intersection, you'll notice that the street to the left and the street to the right both disappear, which is known as two-point perspective. But this weaving doesn't have to be complicated—you can simply play with any shape or object getting smaller. It can even be symbolic; spotlight something you'd like to see reduced in size!

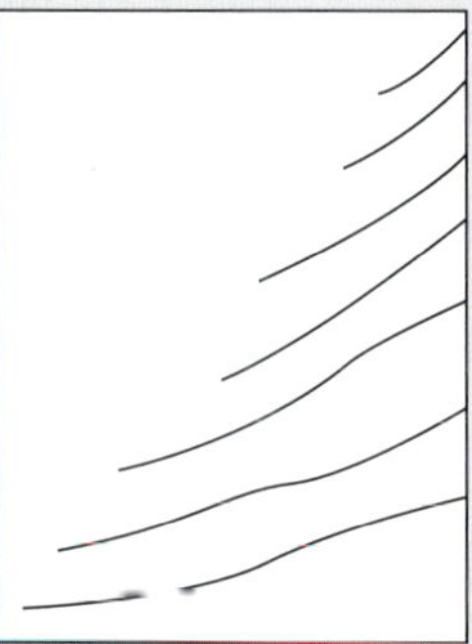

warp

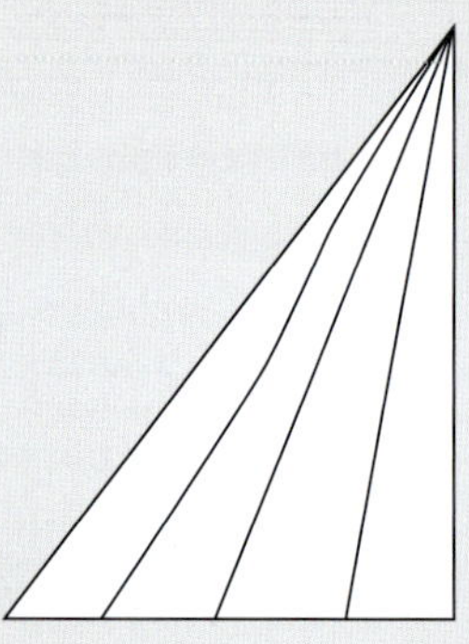

weft

Technique

Add perspective to your weaving. Try starting with an image—a sketch, photo, or print—that has perspective built into it. You can also look up one- and two-point perspective to get ideas.

Materials

- Warp paper: 11" × 8½" Thai marbled paper
- Weft paper: 11" × 8½" solid-colored decorative paper

Instructions

1. Working with the weft sheet, set your ruler between the bottom left corner and the top right corner, and cut the sheet in half diagonally.
2. Place the weft piece on top of the warp, as shown. Draw, with pencil, a faint guideline along the diagonal edge to mark the edge for the warp slits.
3. Cut randomly spaced warp slits on the warp paper, beginning just to the left of the guideline (you'll need extra space for take-up). This photo shows the back of my warp. Note that I cut along the marbled lines, and I also gradually increased the distance between the slits from top to bottom to enhance the perspective effect. Erase the pencil line on the warp paper.
4. Cut the diagonal piece into four strips.
5. Weave, glue ends, and trim, if necessary.

Artists' Variations on the Prompt

One-point perspective

Ron Shaull wove into the contours of the valley floor to increase the "believability" of the perspective. He did several things to enhance the perspective: He cut around the mountain slope shapes, he made the warp slits in the photo gradually wider as they move from background to foreground, and he wove the pink weft strips slightly apart to create the illusion that they are floating.

Two-point perspective

Patricia Minard's piece was inspired by her recollections of large rooms with floor-to-ceiling windows with a garden view.

Weaving 11

Prompt: Routine

Daily Delight

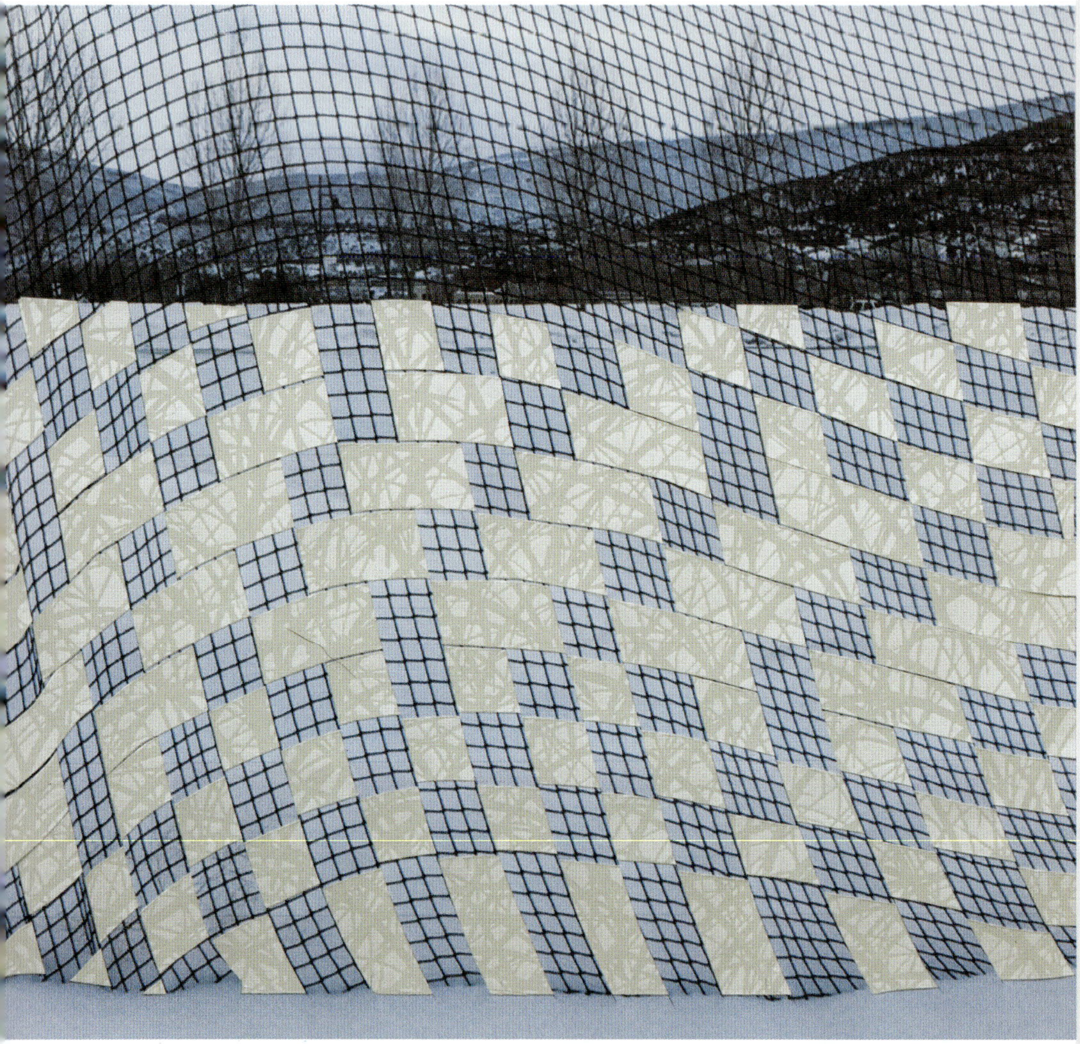

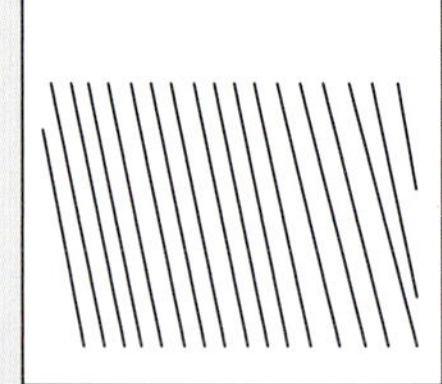

warp

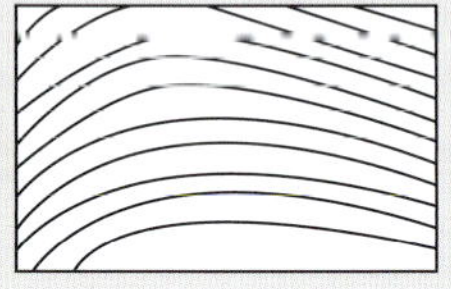

weft

Technique

Find an image or take a photo of something that you can envision weaving into. Create a weaving into the photo or inspired by that photo.

Materials

- Warp paper: 7¾" × 7¾" photo by the author, printed on 32 lb paper
- Weft paper: 4¾" × 7½" decorative paper

You probably have many daily routines—reading, exercising, cooking, knitting, spending time with family. Try incorporating one of your routines into a weaving. Close your eyes and contemplate your daily routines. What stands out? Is there something that relaxes you, despite what the day may bring? Is there something you always look forward to? I walk my dogs along the same route each morning and noticed the way snow collected on a net in the ball field we pass. The grid of the net reminded me of a weaving. I took a photo and used that as a starting point for this weaving.

Instructions

1. Take or find a photo and print it. This will be your warp. Choose a contrasting weft paper.
2. Lay a piece of tracing paper over the warp and tape it in place. Trace the outline of the area you will weave into and then trace along the lines in your photo. This is the pattern for your weft piece.

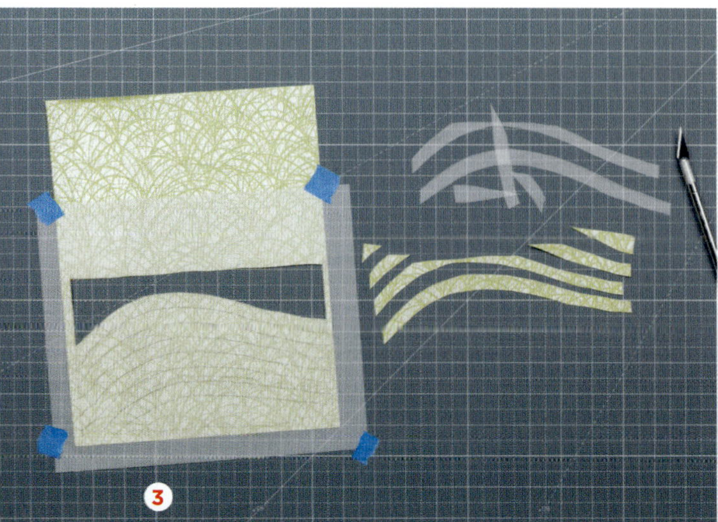

3. Tape the pattern over the weft paper and cut it into strips, keeping them in order on your cutting mat.
4. Cut warp slits into the photo as desired. Note that I cut warp slits and weft strips along existing lines in the photo.
5. Weave the weft strips into the warp. I used an under one/over two pattern that was staggered, but you can see in the final weaving that there are a few strips that are woven under one/over one at the top and bottom of my weaving.
6. Glue ends and trim, if necessary. I trimmed off the white edges of the copier paper to finish my weaving.

Artists' Variations on the Prompt

▲ For the routine prompt, Cynthia Reid printed a photograph of a pile of cinder blocks that she sees routinely on her property, in black and white on copier paper. She wove in a translucent white paper, which obscures some of the holes in the cinder blocks.

► For her routine prompt, Karen Hall wove into a printed image of a toothbrush with very tiny strips. She added color to the background by weaving in deli paper that had been monoprinted with acrylic paint.

Weaving 12

Prompt: Window

Looking Out

Windows come in so many styles and forms, from bay windows to decorative windows like stained glass, where the beauty is the window. Envision a view that you currently have or would love to have and create this weaving with that in mind. One paper represents the window, while the other paper represents the view.

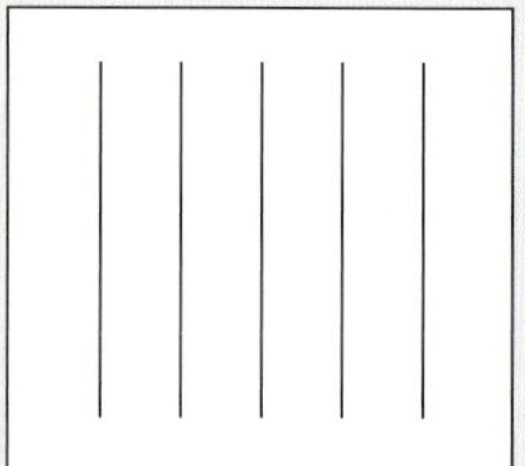

warp

weft

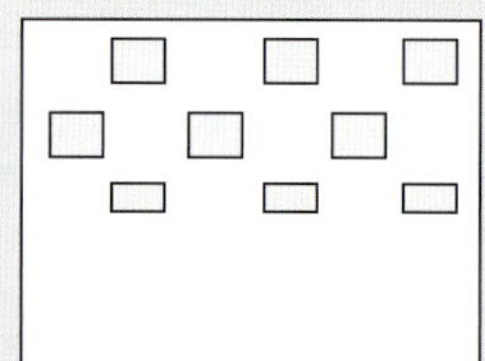

window pattern

Technique

Cut windows in your weaving.

Materials

- Warp paper: Copyright-free image, printed on standard copier paper
- Weft paper: 6" × 7¼" lokta paper with branches print

Instructions

1. Measure the length and width of the image you will weave into and cut the weft paper to that size.
2. Cut vertical slits into the warp paper.
3. Cut the weft piece into horizontal strips.
4. Weave. Then cut windows in the woven sections; see the instructions on page 48.

Note: I cut windows in the top half of the weaving to reveal more of the sky, then partial windows in the central strip to reveal the sky while keeping the landscape covered. The bottom two strips don't have any windows.

2

3

4

Artists' Variations on the Prompt

Davida Feder scanned a magazine page and an upholstery fabric sample and printed them on 24 lb Strathmore paper. After weaving, she cut lots of windows with thin edges.

Cynthia Reid wove sheet music for the song "The Falling Leaves" into a leaf-patterned paper to relate to the title of the song. She cut windows in both papers: in the red leaf-patterned paper to reveal the lyrics of the song, and in the sheet music to highlight the falling leaves.

Weaving 13

Prompt: Direction

Any Way You Like It

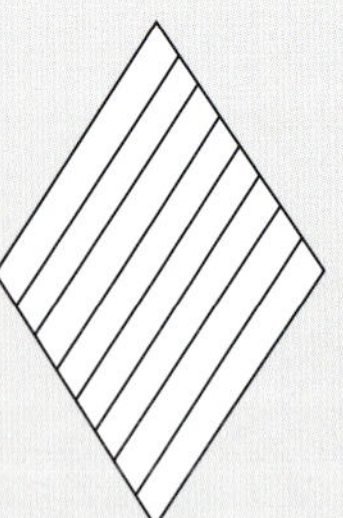

warp

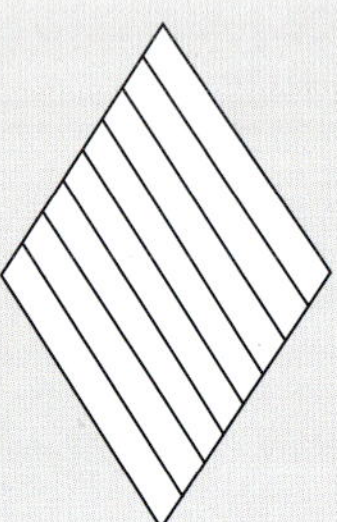

weft

Technique

Weave strips on the diagonal.

Materials

- Warp + weft papers: Two 6" squares of Tant origami paper in different colors

A compass has eight named points, but there's an infinite number of directions between them, just as there's an infinite number of directions your weaving can take. Think about things that move in distinct or different directions. Ideas: an airplane taking off or landing, shooting stars, snow rolling down a hill, fireworks. Formulate an image in your head and create a weaving sparked by that image.

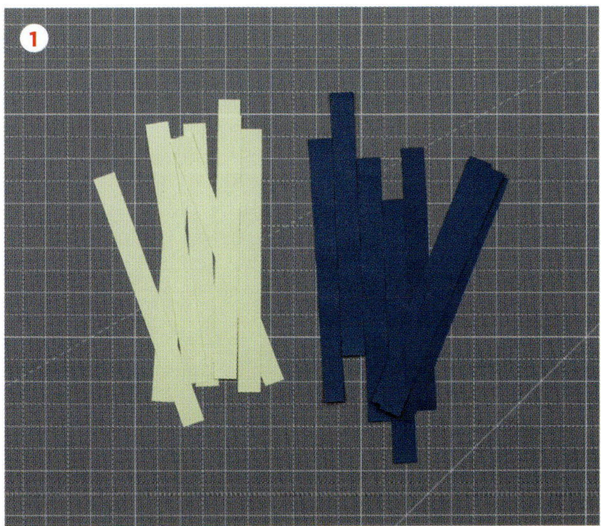

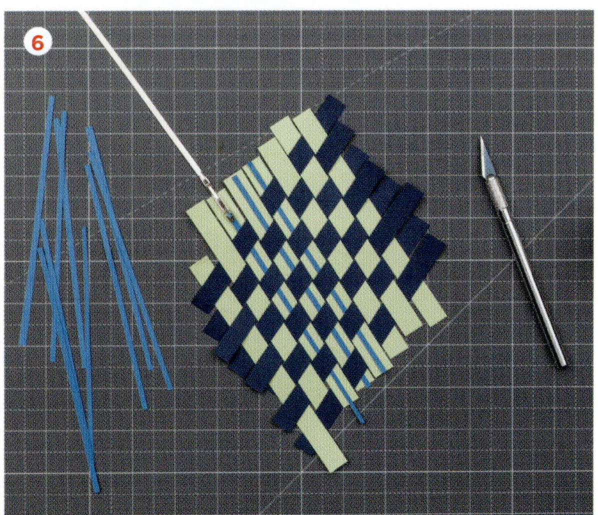

Instructions

1. Cut eight ½" strips out of each 6" square (you will use only a portion of each square). I used a paper trimmer and cut both sets of strips at the same time.
2. Weave from the center out (see page 81), establishing a diagonal pattern with the first couple of strips.
3. Continue weaving until you have used all 16 strips.
4. Push the strips together to eliminate take-up and shape the diamond.
5. Carefully trim excess paper to create a diamond shape, taking care not to dislodge any woven strips.
6. **Optional:** Cut some thin (⅛") strips in a complementary color and use the weaving tool to overweave those into the existing weaving, in one or both directions.
7. Glue ends and trim, as desired.

Artists' Variations on the Prompt

▲ Héloïse Bossard's grandfather was discharged from the army at the end of World War II because of an injury. She cut up his war pension document to create the text strips and made the cuts in the chiyogami paper as small as possible so they look like stitches.

◄ The back of Héloïse Bossard's piece reveals the structure of the weave and the stitchlike slits.

Beverly Frey used straight lines in this weaving to imply curves.
Those strips really are straight!

Weaving 14

Prompt: Circle

Circle in a Square

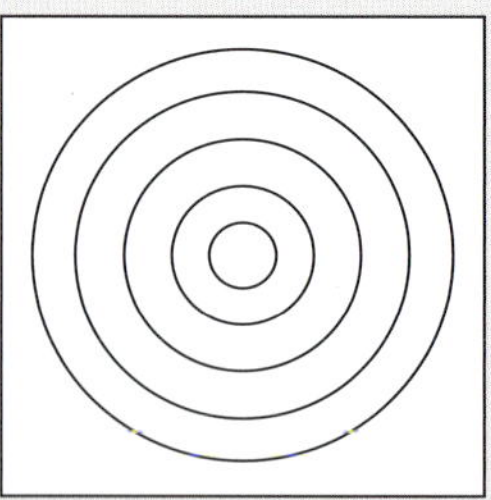

warp

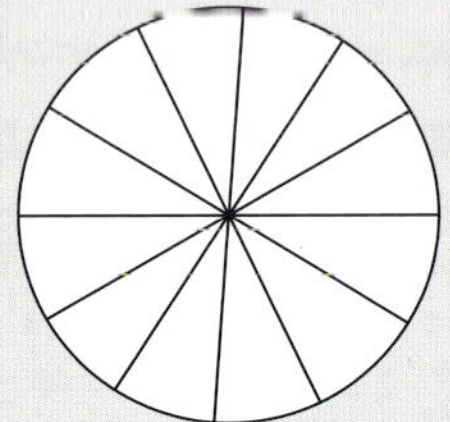

weft

Technique

Practice a target weave.

Materials

- Warp paper: 12" square of textured paper
- Weft paper: 10¼" square of Tairei paper
- Special tool: Circle cutter or compass

The circle is a universal representation of wholeness—because it has no beginning and no end. So many spiritual and energetic symbols, from a variety of cultures, are circular. Think of the yin and yang, a labyrinth, a mandala, or the circle of life. Make a list of circular objects, drawing ideas from both natural and human-made spheres—a wheel, Earth, a ball, the sun, a bull's-eye. Choose one that inspires you and use it as the basis for this weaving.

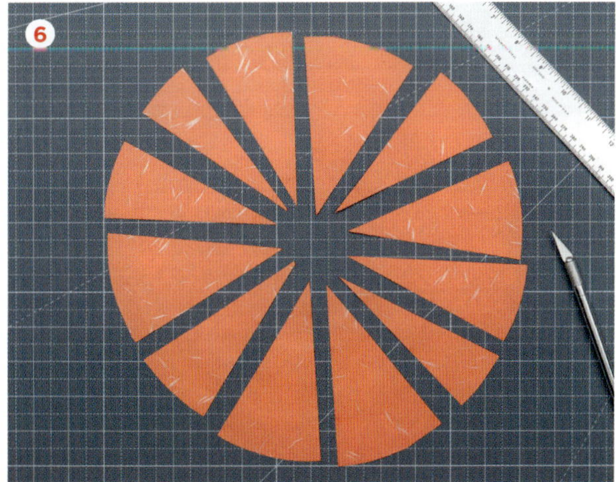

Instructions

1. Create a circular weft piece. In the smaller paper, cut a 10"-diameter (5"-radius) circle using a circle cutter. Alternatively, you can use a ruler to measure and mark the center point of the smaller square, place a compass on the mark, and draw a 10" circle, then cut it out. Mark the centerpoint.
2. Center the circular weft paper on the back side of the warp paper and trace it. Do not cut this circle out—it will serve as a guideline for weaving.
3. Place the circle cutter in the center of the warp piece and set it to cut an 8"-diameter (4"-radius) circle. Cut out the 8" circle.
4. Repeat step 3 to cut 6"-, 4"-, and 2"-diameter circles, each one inside the next.
5. Draft the weft pieces. Draw a line through the center point on the weft circle. Then use a ruler to draw another line that crosses the first one perpendicularly, dividing the circle into quarters. Further divide each quarter into three more pieces. These pie wedges do not have to be the same size, but they must all intersect at the center point.
6. Use a ruler and craft knife to cut out the weft pieces. Keep the pieces in order on the cutting mat, numbering them on the back, if you wish.

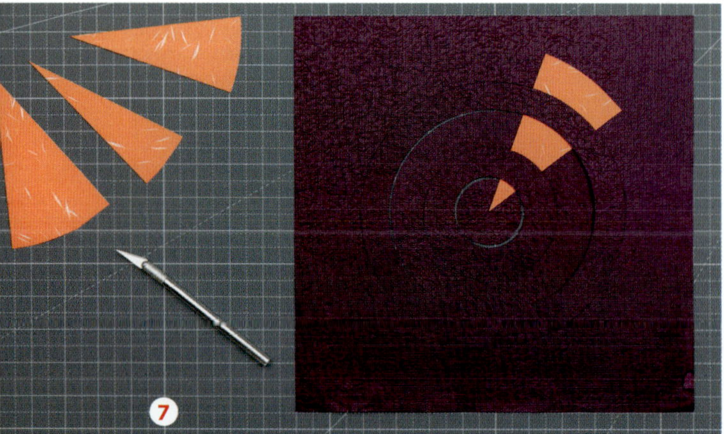
7

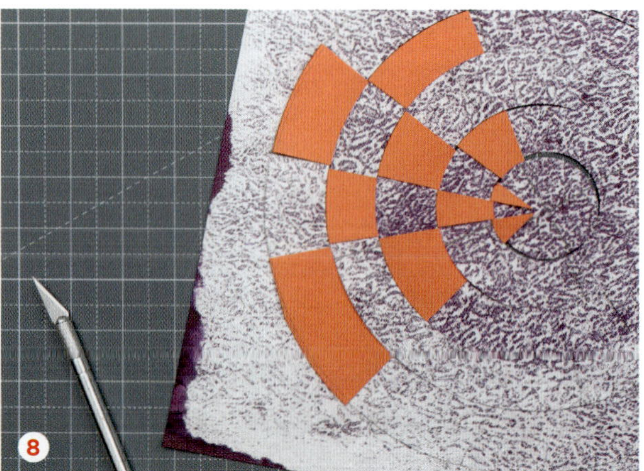
8

10

7. Arrange the concentric circles back into place, as shown, and carefully weave in one wedge-shaped strip.
8. Continue weaving, keeping the strips in order. After you have four or five strips woven, turn the weaving over. Use the outer circle (drawn in pencil on the back) as a guide for lining up the strips. Try to keep the points of the pie wedges in the center. The more you weave, the more difficult it will become to readjust the pieces.
9. If the last strip is too large, simply cut a small wedge-shaped slice off so that it will fit into the weaving. Once you have everything in place, glue ends and trim, if necessary.
10. If you don't like how the points of your pie wedges line up in the center, simply cut a small circle to glue on top of them!

Artists' Variations on the Prompt

► Susan Buhler-Maki trimmed the outer warp into a circle instead of a square and used text to draw the viewer in to find the words.

► Here's another approach to circle weaving. Héloïse Bossard wove straight strips strategically to show off the warp rings.

Weaving 15

Prompt: Concentric

Inside Out

warp

weft

Technique

This weaving is a natural progression from the previous target-weave prompt, but the weft strips are treated differently. Cut the warp and weft into the same shape, and then cut the warp into concentric shapes and the weft into strips.

Materials

- Warp paper: 6" square of origami paper
- Weft paper: 6" square of Italian print

Concentric layers abound in the world. From chocolate-covered, nougat-covered caramel to Russian matryoshka dolls (nesting dolls), you can find many real-life examples of items with concentric layers. As an artist, what kinds of things can you imagine having embedded layers? Have some fun with this weaving and create something uniquely your own.

Instructions

1. Draw a heart-shaped outline on the warp paper. (I used the method I learned as a kid: Fold the warp paper in half and draw half a heart on the centerfold. Cut the folded sheet and then unfold it.)

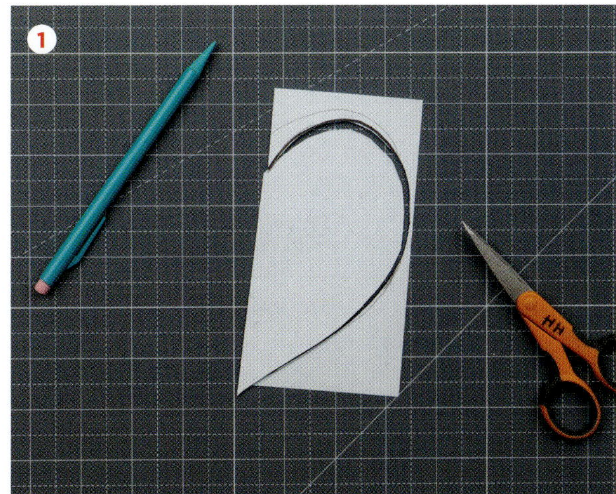
1

2

2. Fold the weft and warp papers in half. Trace the folded warp paper onto the back side of the folded weft paper. Cut out a second heart and set aside.
3. Draw three concentric half hearts on the folded warp paper and cut them out with a craft knife or scissors. Unfold and reassemble.

I always like to flip my weaving over to look at the back. Sometimes it looks more interesting—or in this case, more graphic—than the front.

4. Cut the weft piece into ½"-wide vertical strips, keeping them in order.
5. Start weaving in the center, which will hold everything together best. I wove two central strips vertically in an alternating over/under fashion. Then I worked my way to the right, came back to the center, and worked my way from the center out to the left. You can simply lift the right and left sides of concentric hearts and slip weft strips in sideways.
6. Glue ends and trim, if necessary.

Artists' Variations on the Prompt

◂ Ron Shaull cut his star-shaped red warp into four concentric shapes. Then he cut a 5½" square piece of zebra-patterned wallpaper into ¼" strips to make the points and angles of the star shapes pop (his first attempt with thicker ½" strips didn't work as well).

◂ For my concentric weaving, I drew a small triangular shape in the center of the green paper and then drew concentric shapes around it. The blue sheet was cut into wavy horizontal strips.

Weaving 16

Prompt: Ephemera

Those Were the Days

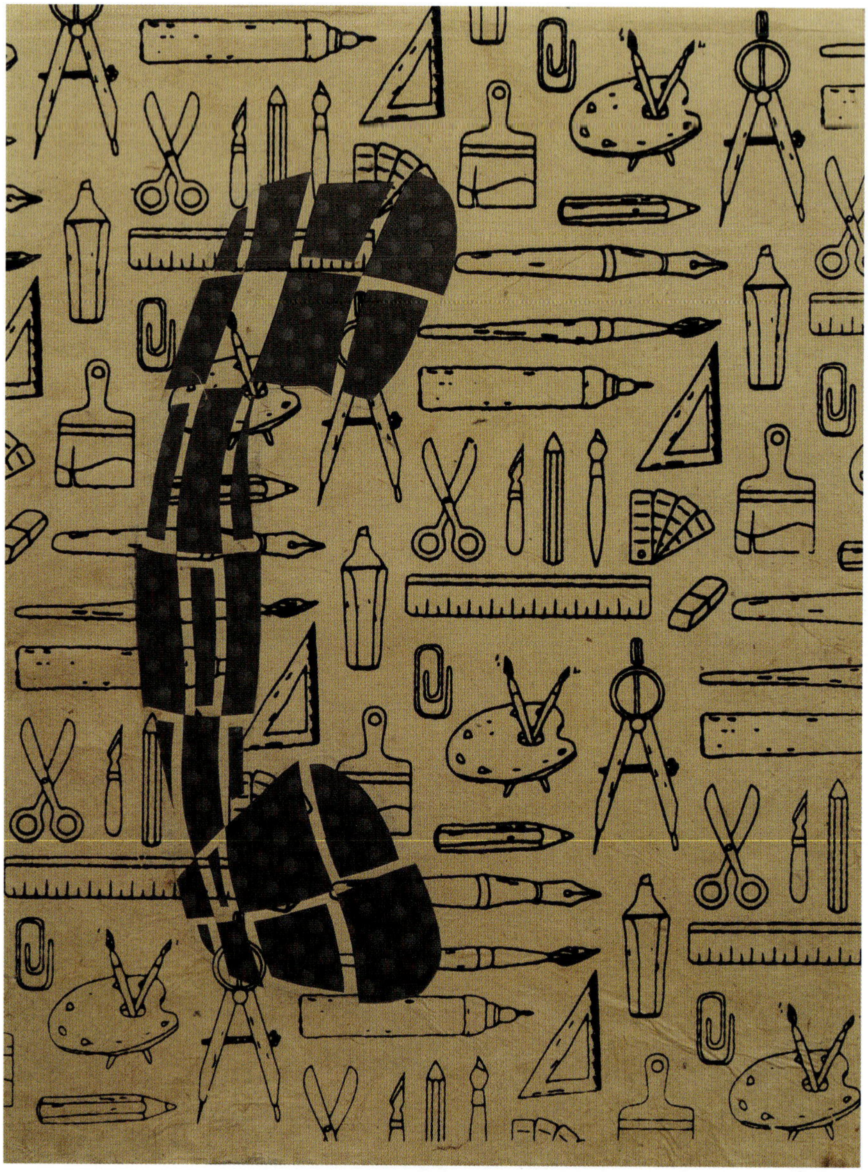

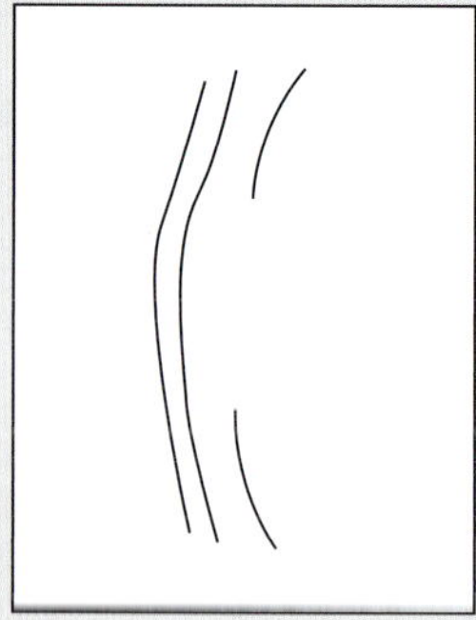

warp

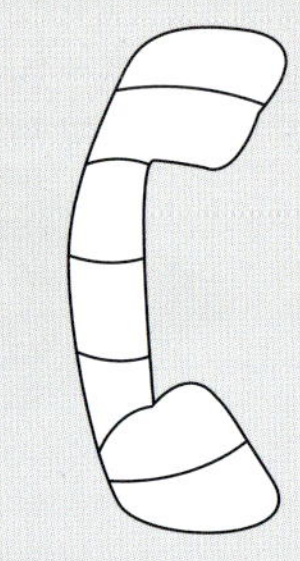

weft

Technique

Weave a simple shape into the warp.

Materials

- Warp paper: 11½" × 8½" lokta paper with art supplies pattern
- Weft paper: 8" × 3" machine-made paper with polka-dot pattern

Souvenirs. Keepsakes. Family photos. We all have them, and there are many printed items that might remind you of times gone by, like the paper I used in my sample weaving. Perhaps you have a vintage magazine you could take a page from, or an image you drew when you were a child. Be sure to make a photocopy of anything of value and use the copy—not the original—in your weaving.

Instructions

1. Find a nostalgic shape (or any shape). I printed out this image of an old telephone and cut out the receiver to create a pattern for the weft. Use the weft pattern to cut out the shape from your weft paper.
2. Place the weft piece (in reverse) on the back of the warp paper and trace the outline.
3. Cut vertical slits into the warp.
4. Cut the weft piece into horizontal strips approximately 1" wide.

5. Weave and glue ends. Note that I wove from the back so that I could use the outline of the receiver to position my strips.
6. Cut windows, if desired, to help reveal the weft shape.

Artists' Variations on the Prompt

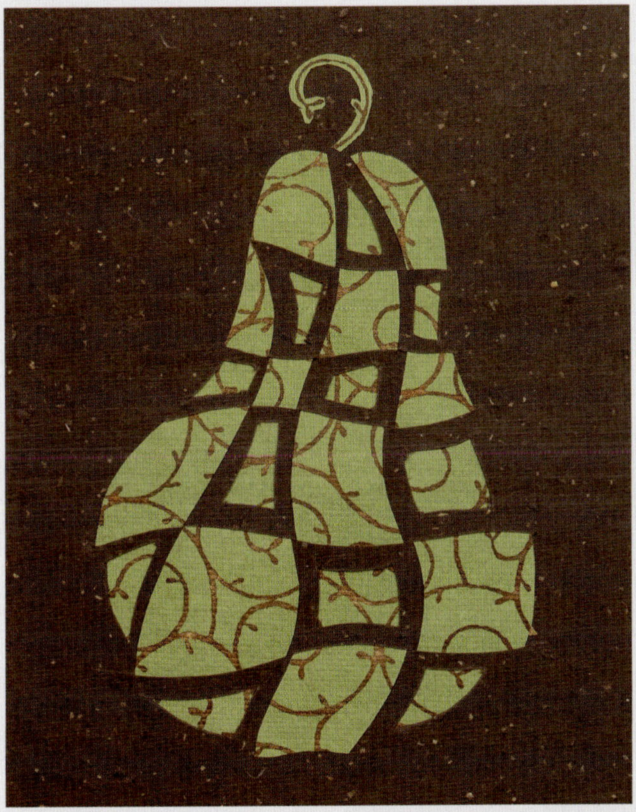

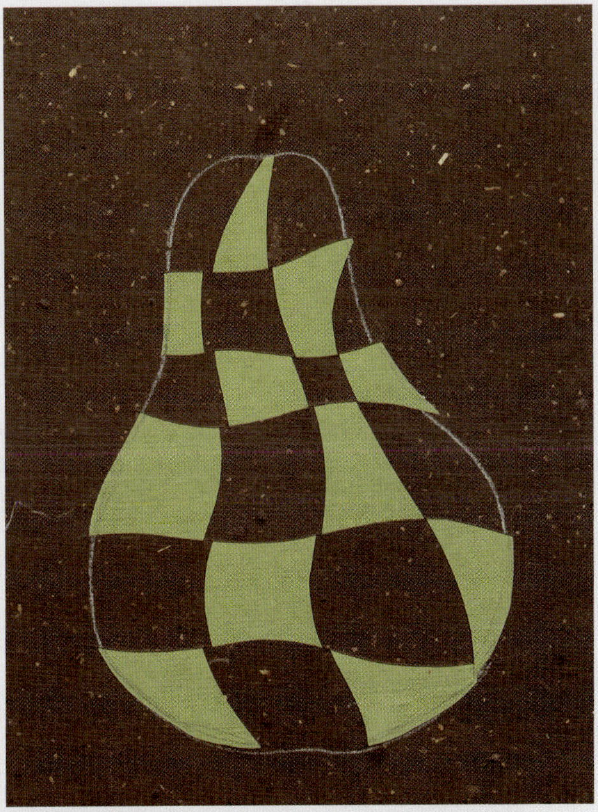

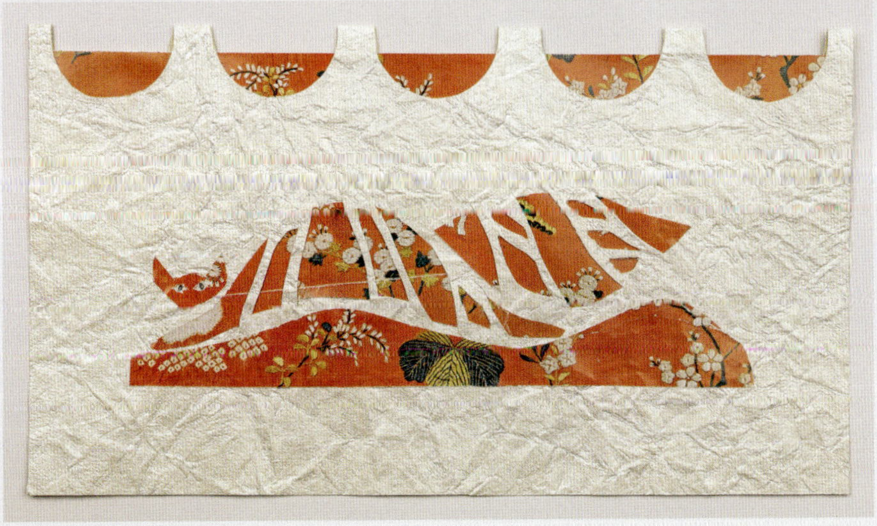

▲ For the ephemera prompt, Cathy Moore wove a familiar fruit and cut windows to define the shape. The stem was collaged onto the piece. (Here you see the front and back of the weaving).

◀ This design celebrates the historic Foxden Press at Cornell College in Mount Vernon, Iowa. Kirilka Stavreva wove two separate shapes into the warp: the fox's body and tail. Then she cut some windows. The fox's head and the undulating blooming prairie are collage elements. The top edge of the weaving is folded over and punched, which allows for hanging.

Weaving 17

Prompt: Silhouette

Standing Out

When you look at a well-composed photo, you see the subject in the foreground and a backdrop, building, view, or other secondary objects in the background. That's the principle you're exploring with this weaving—defining a subject, so it stands out from the rest of the piece. Let your mind be the lens of a camera and find a subject to use for this weaving. A shadow on the wall or ceiling at night might be an excellent place to start.

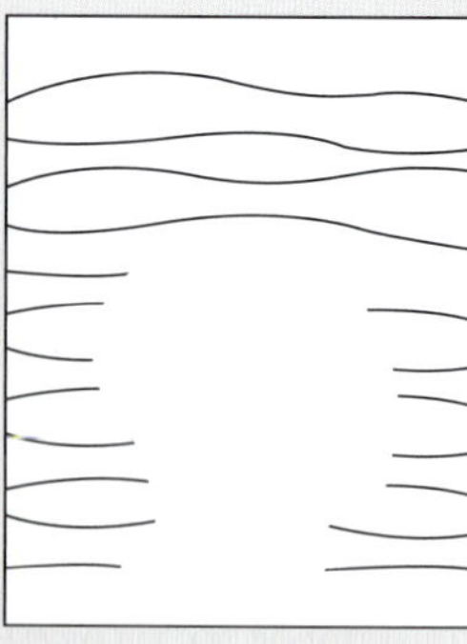

warp

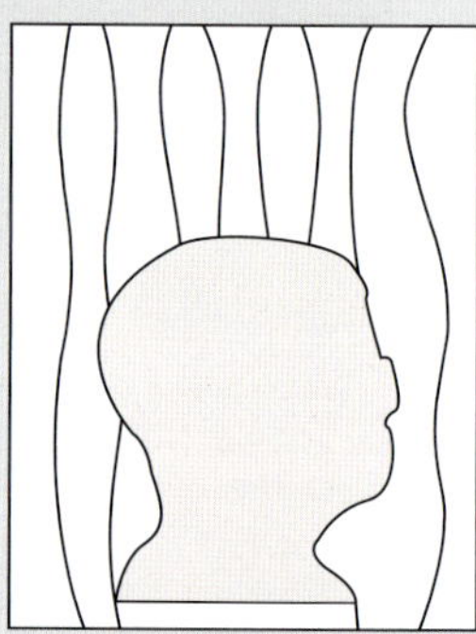

weft

Technique

Weave into negative space.

Materials

- Warp paper: 11" × 8½" flocked paper
- Weft paper: 11" × 8½" Thai kozo paper
- Stencil paper: 11" × 8½" cardstock

Tip: To create a silhouette of a person, have your subject stand against a solid-colored wall and take a photo of them in profile. Print the photo and cut out the silhouette.

Instructions

1. Cut a silhouette or another shape out of a piece of cardstock to create a silhouette pattern.
2. Trace the pattern onto the back of your weft paper, in the position where you want it. Cut out the silhouette shape and remove it.
3. Before cutting the weft piece into strips, place it on top of the back side of your warp paper and trace the silhouette shape.
4. Mark the vertical strips on the weft paper. (Use a white pencil if your paper is dark.) Then cut the strips.
5. On the warp paper, mark the horizontal strips and slits around the silhouette (do not mark any cuts in the silhouette). Then cut the strips and slits in the warp paper.

Warp (blue paper) and weft (beige paper), as seen from the back

6. Weave weft strips into the warp, around the silhouette shape (I worked on the back side of my weaving).
7. Glue ends and trim, if necessary.
8. Cut windows into the weft paper around the silhouette to accentuate the shape, if desired.

Artists' Variations on the Prompt

▶ Shirley Cook used a gel plate monoprint for the background paper and wove a multilayered brayer roll-off paper into the positive space. Note how she cut windows along the sides to accentuate the vase shape.

▼ Rebecca Winter wove into the negative space using ¼" strips to accentuate the teacup. She carefully cut the warp strips along the edge of the teacup, so the weft strips slipped behind the warp along the curves of the cup. Looking at the back of her weaving, you can see how she trimmed the strips behind the teacup as she wove.

Weaving 18

Prompt: Highlight

Center Stage

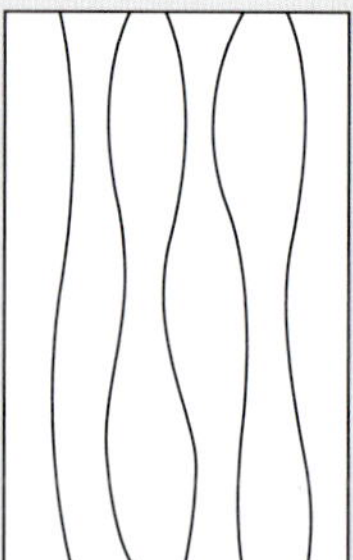

warp

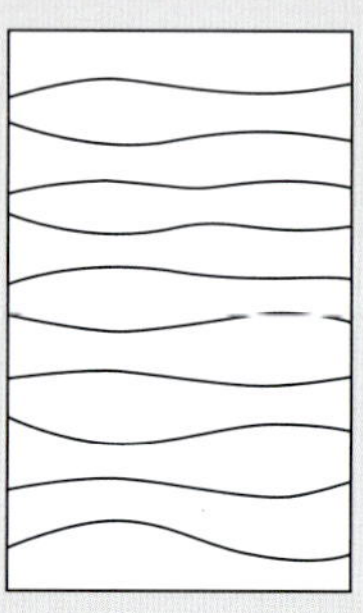

weft

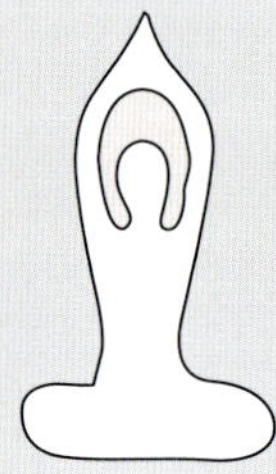

stencil

Technique

Cut windows in both papers on one side of your weaving to define a shape.

Materials

- Warp paper: 11" × 6¾" decorative paper
- Weft paper: 11" × 6¾" elephant hide paper
- Stencil paper: 11" × 8½" cardstock

Now that you've mastered defining foreground subject matter, you'll tackle a unique method of highlighting a subject. Think of a simply shaped object to use—a still life, like a vase or a bowl, would work, but anything will do! Jot down some ideas and decide what the focus of your weaving will be.

Instructions

1. Cut the warp and weft papers into curved strips.
2. Plain-weave the two together and glue the ends.
3. Print, draw, or trace a shape onto the cardstock and cut it out.
4. Place the cutout stencil in position on top of your weaving and tape in place.
5. Trace the stencil onto your weaving with a pencil.

▲ The cut-out shape is revealed in the illuminated view of the project.

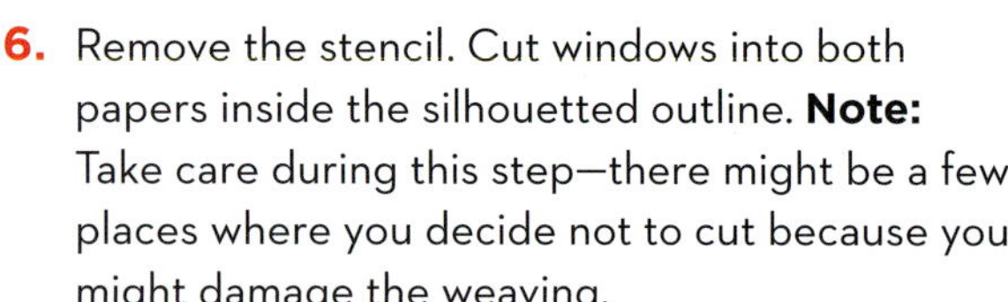

6. Remove the stencil. Cut windows into both papers inside the silhouetted outline. **Note:** Take care during this step—there might be a few places where you decide not to cut because you might damage the weaving.
7. Erase pencil marks.
8. Hold your weaving up to the light. You might be surprised by the effect.

Artists' Variations on the Prompt

▲ Susan Buhler-Maki cut strategic windows to depict the playfulness of a cat hiding.

▲ The papers you choose can hinder or help a design show through. In my first attempt, with two papers that both had patterns and texture, I could barely see the image of the figure.

▼ If you don't succeed, try, try again! This is Karen Hall's third attempt at the highlight prompt—the paper patterns and values in the first two left the shape barely visible. She cut windows into both warp and weft papers to make the shape appear.

Weaving 19

Prompt: Symbol

What Do You Stand For?

What mark or symbol resonates with you? Is it a heart for love, a dove for peace, an owl for wisdom? Pick one to work with. If there's more than one that has a particular meaning to you, no worries—you can always return to this style of weaving.

warp

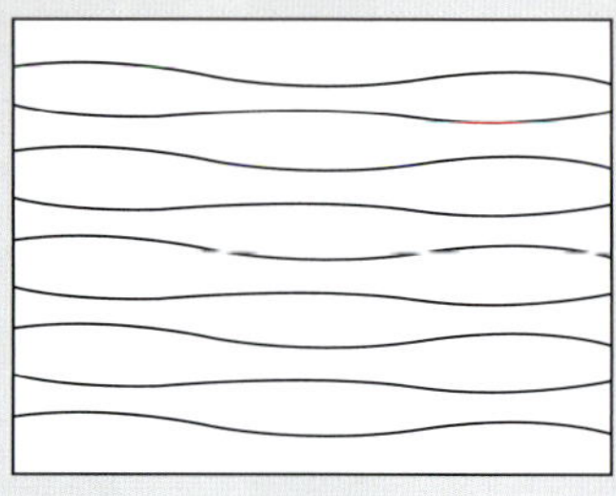
weft

Technique

Reveal a shape with the weaving structure.

Materials

- Warp paper: 9" × 10½" section of a map of Colorado
- Weft paper: 9" × 10½" logwood-dyed artist-made paper
- Printed downloadable warp template (see link on page 210)

Instructions

1. Print or trace the warp template onto your warp paper.
2. Cut along all solid lines.
3. Cut the weft paper into horizontal strips.
4. Weave this pattern from the middle up, and then go back and weave from the middle down. You might need to change the weaving structure at the top and bottom of the yin-yang symbol to define the shape.
5. Glue ends and trim, if necessary.

Artists' Variations on the Prompt

▲ Cathy Moore wove three contrasting papers. She cut a set of both white and orange weft strips at the same time and then wove every other row in the opposite color.

◀ This weaving was simpler than it looks. Think of the dove as a strip. I cut the dove (the positive space) out of the red paper and kept it in "the frame" (the negative space) in the same paper. Then I cut ¼" strips of light green and wove them over and under the dove.

Weaving 20

Prompt: Winding

Around & Around

I enjoy knitting, so when I think about “winding,” I immediately think of yarn. We’re exploring spirals in this project. What comes to your mind? Spools of thread? An old clock or watch? A cyclone? A yo-yo? A rope? Perhaps a maze? Amaze yourself with your selection.

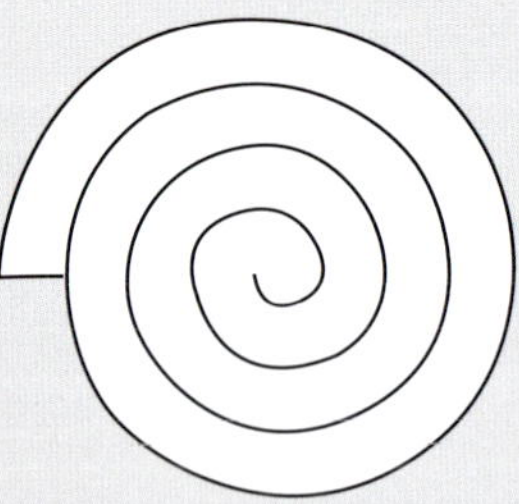

warp

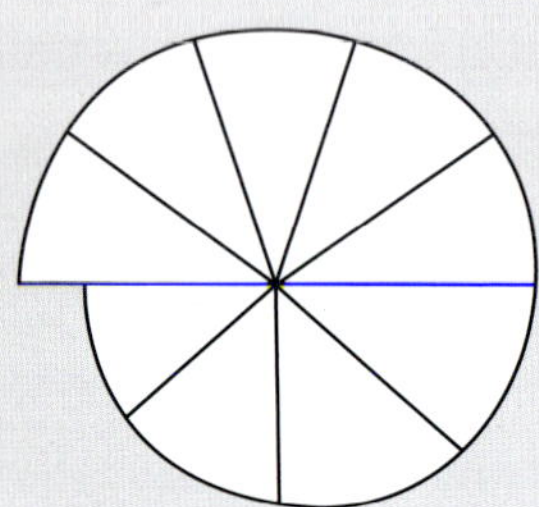

weft

Technique

Cut your warp into a spiral.

Materials

- Warp paper: 8¼" square of decorative paper
- Weft paper: 8¼" square of origami paper
- Printed downloadable warp and weft templates (see link on page 210)

Tip: The weft piece must be cut into an odd number of pieces in order to weave together properly.

Instructions

1. Print the warp template and tape it to the warp paper. Carefully cut out the spiral.
2. Print the weft template and tape it to the weft paper. Cut out the weft piece, and then cut it into pie-shaped wedges.
3. Weave the weft pieces into the warp spiral.
4. If the last strip doesn't fit, trim off a thin wedge from the outer edge to the center point. (You can also trim the curve of the outside of the wedge if it sticks out too far.)
5. Glue ends and trim, if necessary.

Artists' Variations on the Prompt

▶ (left) Therese Lennert has been in awe of the shape and texture of ammonites ever since her father found two in their backyard when she was a child. Circular and spiral weaving revived her fondness for them, and she tried to capture their unique pattern in this weaving.

▶ (right) Lisa Merkin highlights the beauty of the Fibonacci sequence in nature. She created a tracing paper pattern for the arc shape and cut five arcs to make weft strips. She cut slits in an image of aloe and wove the arc strips through them. She glued on a few circles to finish the piece.

Weaving 21

Prompt: Crossing

Back to the Strip

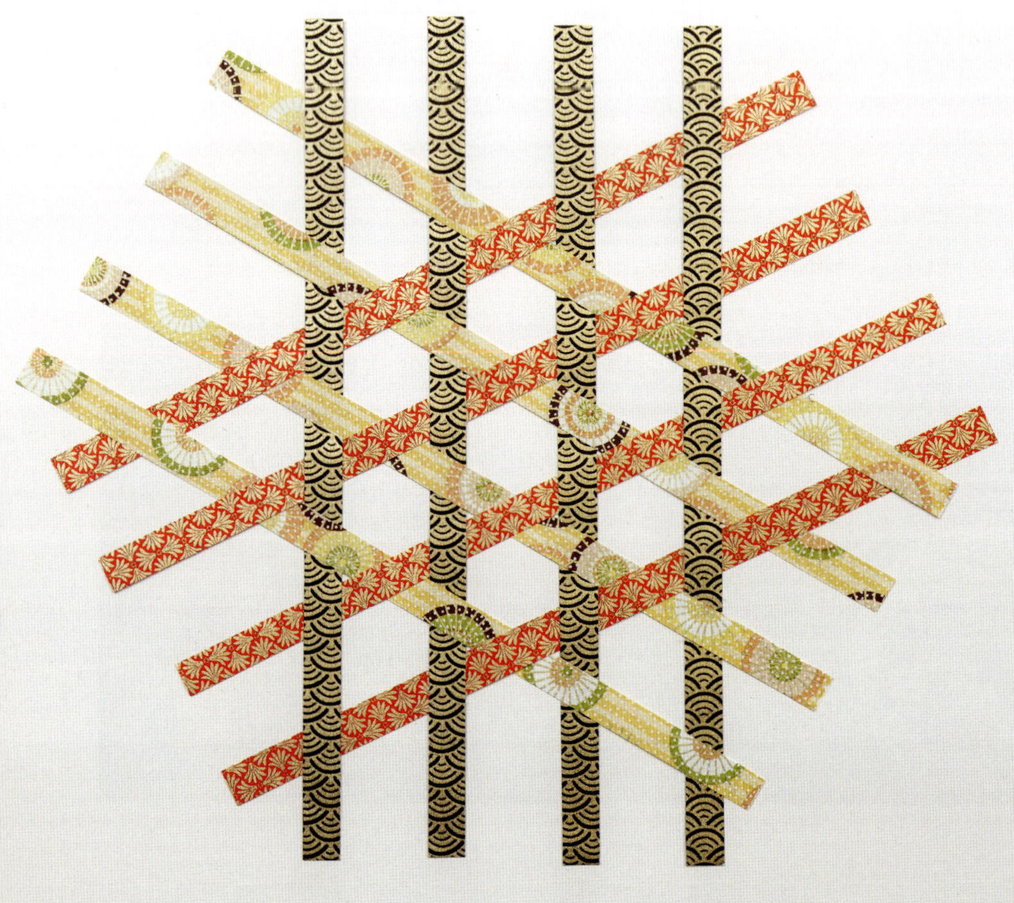

warp

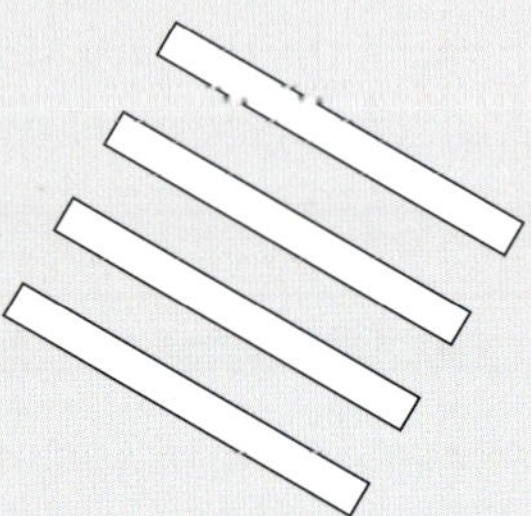

weft #1

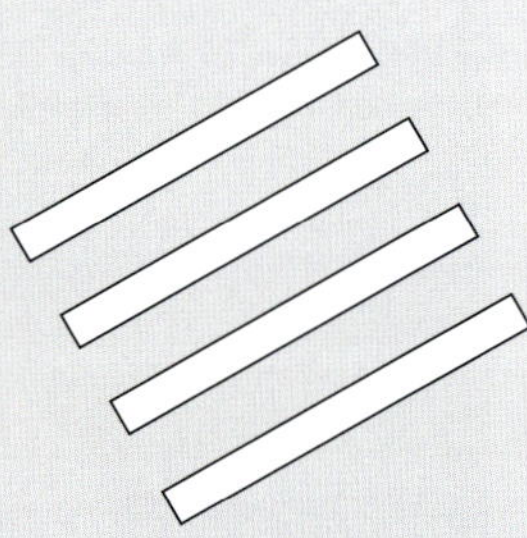

weft #2

Technique

Practice hexagonal weaving.

Materials

- Papers: 4 strips each of 3 chiyogami papers, all cut to 12" × ½"
- 14" × 12" piece of foam core or cardboard
- 24 straight pins or removable tape
- Printed downloadable template (see link on page 210)
- Special tool: Weaving tool (see Resources, page 210)

The challenge here is to weave vertical and diagonal strips into an open weave. What could those strips be? A grid of roads with intersections? Strips of grass that surround garden plots? Or are they simply fun colors, like the sample weaving I made? Whatever you choose, remember that you'll be seeing through to the background you place the weaving on, which can add to the beauty of the piece. This is a basket-weave pattern, which doesn't really have warp and weft, but rather strips that interlock.

Tips

- The weaving tool came in handy on this one.
- I used a pair of tweezers to lift the strips while weaving.

Instructions

1. Print the template on copier paper and tape it on top of a sheet of foam core or cardboard that is a few inches larger than the template.
2. Lay four matching strips out vertically, on top of the vertical lines on the template, and pin (or tape) them in place.
3. Lay a second set of matching strips on top of the first set, at a 60-degree angle to the vertical strips, as shown. Pin (or tape) in place.
4. Weave in the third set of strips as follows: Each strip weaves under the vertical set and over the diagonal set at an opposing 60-degree diagonal. Notice the triangle junctures that are created as you weave. Readjust and remove pins as necessary while weaving.
5. Tidy the strips, rotating them as needed so that all triangles are interlocked and you see hexagons in the negative space.
6. Spot-glue the interlacements around the perimeter of your weaving.
7. Cut ends into points, if desired (see example on page 139).
8. Place the finished weaving on a contrasting-colored paper to give it even more pop.

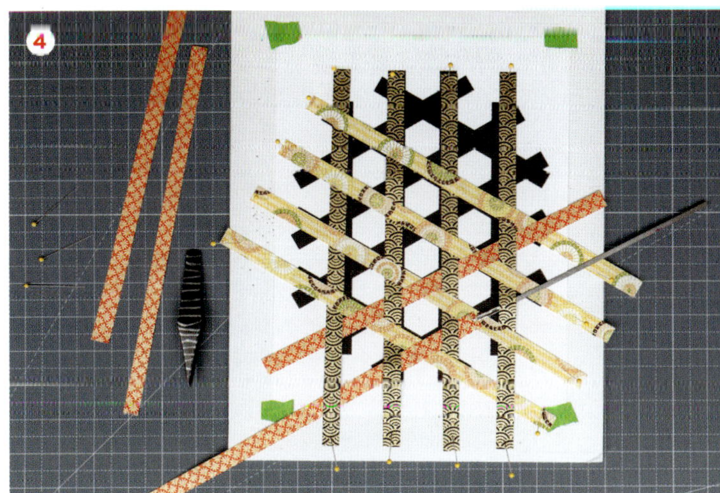

Artists' Variations on the Prompt

Judy Jacques wove an adaptation of a chair-caning pattern. Notice that the negative space is octagonal in this weave.

Kristi Galbraith used strips cut from various paper scraps and glued the final weaving to the front of a blank greeting card.

Weaving 22

Prompt: Treasure

Hidden Gems

Paper weaving enables you to play with dimension. In this project, I created a grid of six sections that are woven together, each with its own treasure revealed by opening a door or a window. You may choose to reveal photos, designs, different colors, secret messages, or pieces of an image. This type of weaving can easily be customized and makes a great gift.

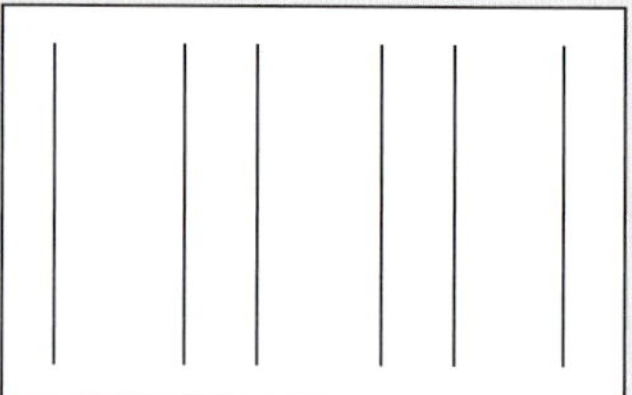

warp

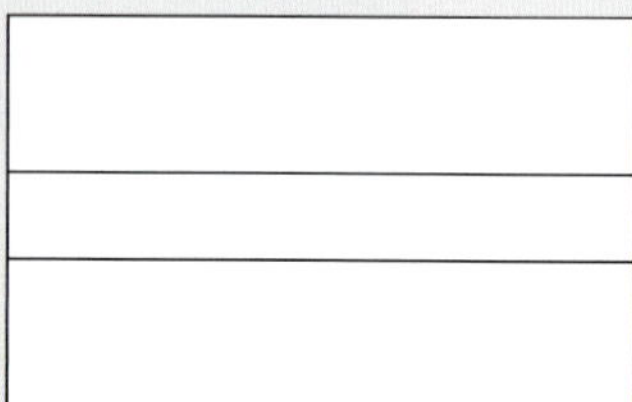

weft

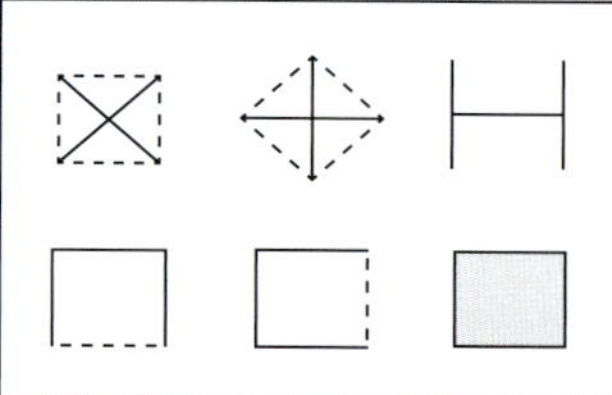

window-cutting guide

Technique

Create window flaps and doors, and tuck treasures inside. (Karen Krieger participated in Weave Through Winter several times and came up with this inventive technique for slipping treasures in between woven window sections.)

Materials

- Warp paper: 4½" × 6½" silver mulberry paper
- Weft paper: 3½" × 6½" mingei paper
- Treasures: 1⅜" squares of Indian artist-made prints
- Special tool: Weaving tool (optional; see Resources, page 210)

Instructions

1. Prepare your warp slits, weft strips, and treasures.
2. Weave the weft strips into the warp slits.
3. Glue ends and trim, if necessary.

4. Slip a cutting mat between the layers at each woven section and cut a variety of windows and doors.
5. Slip treasures behind the windows and doors and spot-glue them in place.

Artists' Variations on the Prompt

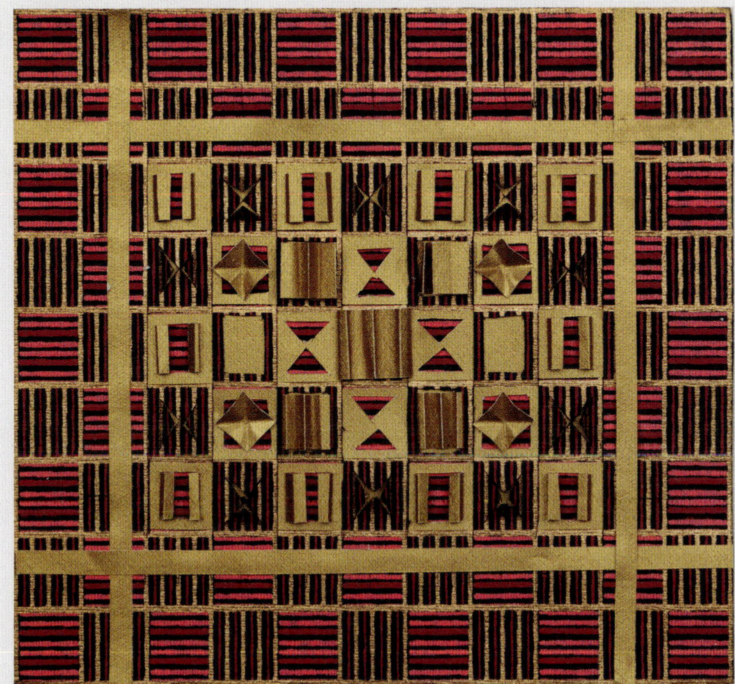

The windows with flaps give Meredith Johanson's weaving an interesting dimension and texture (see detail on pages 144–145).

Karen Krieger created several 2D weavings, cut windows, slipped inserts behind the windows, and hand-stitched around the windows and between each woven section. The weavings were then stitched and transformed into a 3D shape. The piece illustrates the churning emotions that rippled through the world during COVID-19.

Meredith Johanson cut a variety of window flaps and added dimensional elements by folding them. Some of the windows even look like they have shutters (detail; see page 143).

Weaving 23

Prompt: Waves

That's Very Fluttering

warp

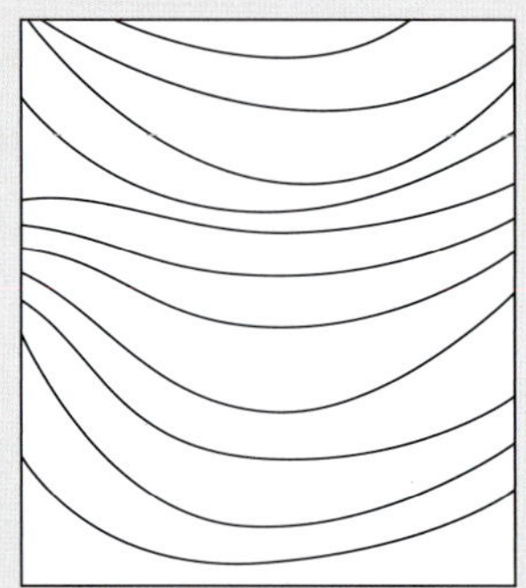

weft

Your choice of paper is key for this one. A paper with a wavy design will look awesome. Consider an image of wavy hair, a wavy pattern that you draw or doodle yourself, something wavy in nature (like the tree bark in my example), a photo of a stormy sky, or a sound wave. It can be dreamy or technical—and the waves don't have to be even. In fact, the more uneven they are, the more interesting your weaving will be.

Technique

Cut along existing lines in a paper or image. Sometimes it helps to lay a piece of tracing paper over an image to sketch out the cut lines for the warp and/or weft strips, so that they end up in the right place.

Materials

- Warp paper: 9½" × 8" detail photo of tree bark
- Weft paper: 9¾" × 8" Tarasen paper with grid pattern

Instructions

1. Print a wavy image onto a sheet of paper.
2. Cut along the prominent wavy lines in your image to create your warp.
3. Make a weft template, with tracing paper, if desired. Place it on top of the weft paper and cut through both layers. Alternatively, simply cut random weft strips.
4. Weave.
5. Glue ends and trim, if necessary.

Artists' Variations on the Prompt

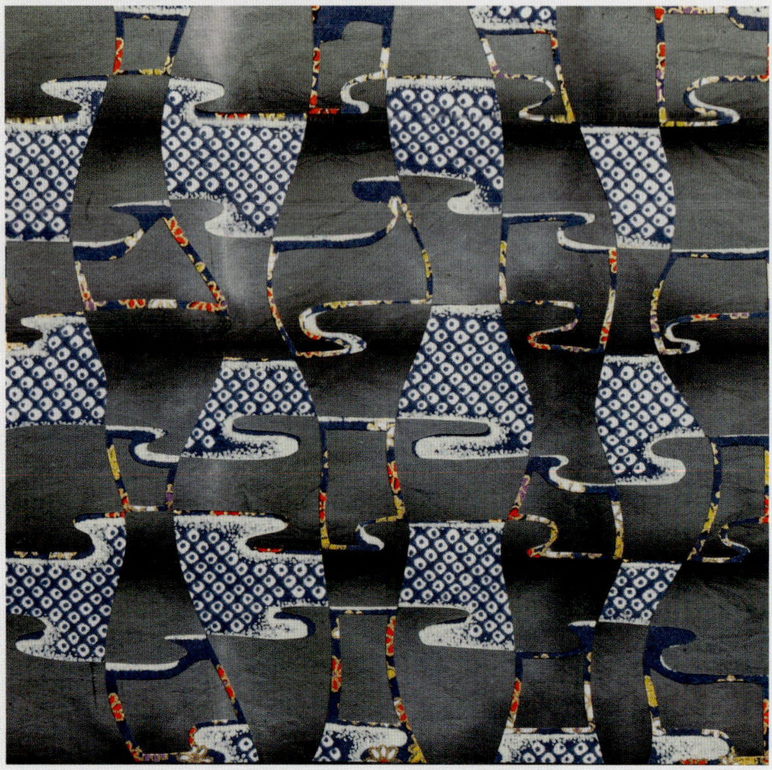

▲ Héloïse Bossard used tracing paper to transfer the shape of wavy clouds onto a gray Japanese paper and then cut that paper along those lines. She cut curvy strips in chiyogami paper and carefully wove them into the gray paper.

► The back side of the weaving shows off her wavy weaving structure.

Sarah Morgan wove blue glitter paper into an architectural drawing from her mother's 1943 college art history notebook. She cut along the existing lines in the drawing to create an arch warp.

Weaving 24

Prompt: Light

All Will Be Revealed

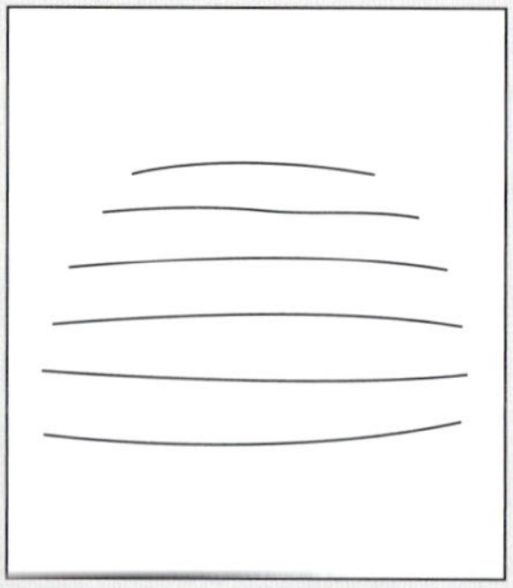

warp

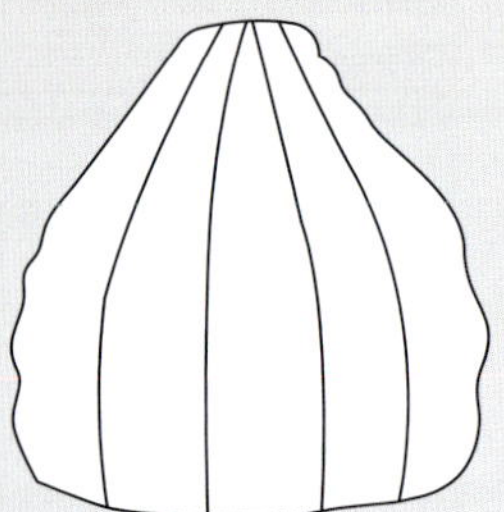

weft

Technique

Make a weaving that requires illumination by cutting windows.

Materials

- Warp paper: 10" × 8" printout or photocopy of an image you wish to illuminate on translucent paper
- Weft paper: 7" square of chiyogami paper

Light can add dimension to artwork. This is also true for woven paper pieces; held up to light, they can take on a glow similar to stained glass. Here you'll be cutting windows again, but your windows will be illuminated this time, revealing details that aren't seen when the weaving is resting on a table or hung on a wall. Try playing with what is revealed. For example, perhaps you can see certain aspects of your weaving only when you put a light behind it.

Instructions

1. Print an image you wish to illuminate onto a sheet of translucent paper; this is your warp.
2. Trace the outline of your shape, using tracing paper, if desired, and mark lines where you will cut vertical strips approximately 1" wide to create a weft template.
3. Place the weft template on top of the weft paper and cut through both layers. Cut the weft piece into vertical strips.
4. Cut horizontal slits into the warp sheet—I cut along the visible horizontal lines in the lantern.

5. Weave, then glue ends.
6. Cut windows (I cut windows into each woven section on the decorative paper on the front side of my weaving).
7. Hold your weaving up to the light!

Artists' Variations on the Prompt

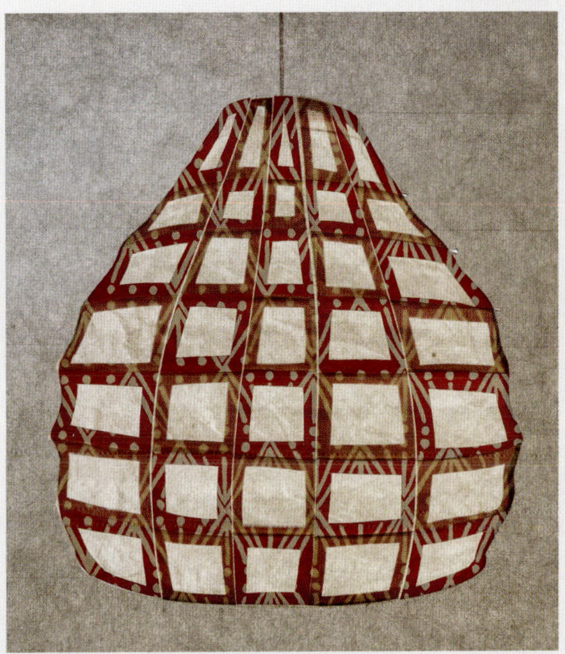

I created the same weaving with a different weft paper. I also cut windows into the weft paper on both sides of the weaving, to create a different illuminated effect.

Beverly Frey used a photo she took at Devils Tower National Monument in Wyoming as a window-cutting guide. She cut windows around the imagery to reveal the scene shown at right when the weaving is backlit.

Weaving 25

Prompt: Layer

What's Under There?

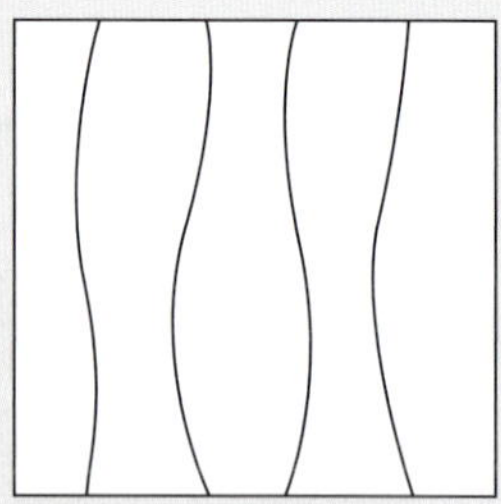
warp

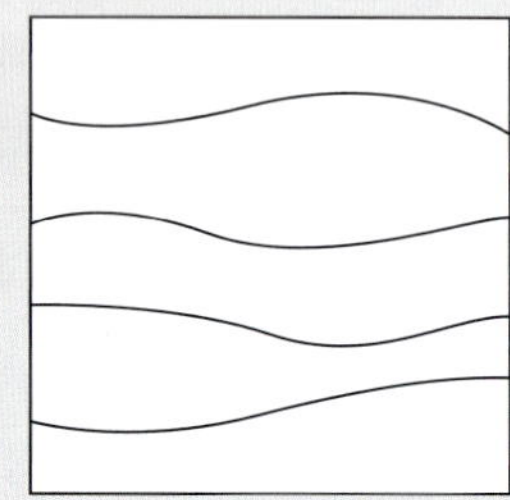
weft

Technique

Cut windows in both layers of paper.

Materials

- Warp paper: 6" square of blue Tairei paper
- Weft paper: 6" square of orange decorative paper
- 6" square of backing paper (optional)

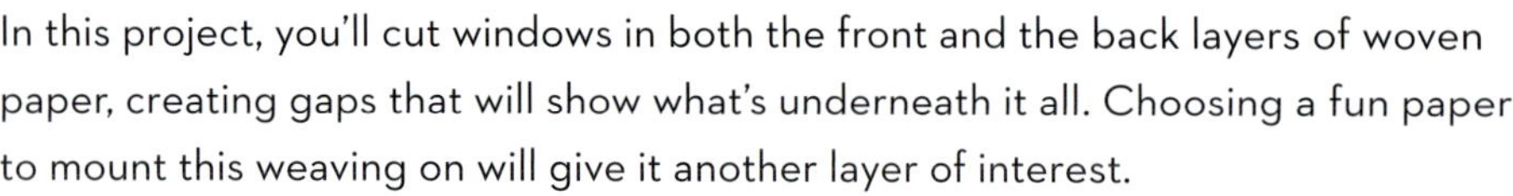

In this project, you'll cut windows in both the front and the back layers of woven paper, creating gaps that will show what's underneath it all. Choosing a fun paper to mount this weaving on will give it another layer of interest.

Instructions

1. Cut the warp and weft papers into curved strips.
2. Create a plain weave, then glue ends and trim. **Note:** Place a piece of scrap paper behind your weaving to catch excess glue.
3. Cut one layer of windows into every woven section, using a piece of flexible cutting mat between the layers.
4. Working on a cutting mat, cut smaller windows in the bottom layer of every woven section.
5. Mount your weaving on a backing paper, if desired.

Artists' Variations on the Prompt

Meredith Johanson's thin windows create an intriguing layered effect that invites you to enjoy the view in her backing paper.

Suellen Meyer went through a dozen possibilities before choosing this black-and-gold wheat sheaf paper for the third layer, which makes this piece dance. Both layers of windows follow the curves of her warp and weft strips.

Weaving 26

Prompt: Variety

A Little Bit of This, a Little Bit of That

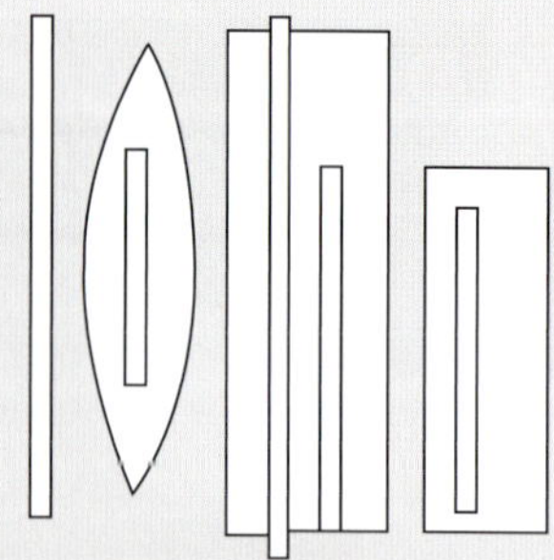

warp

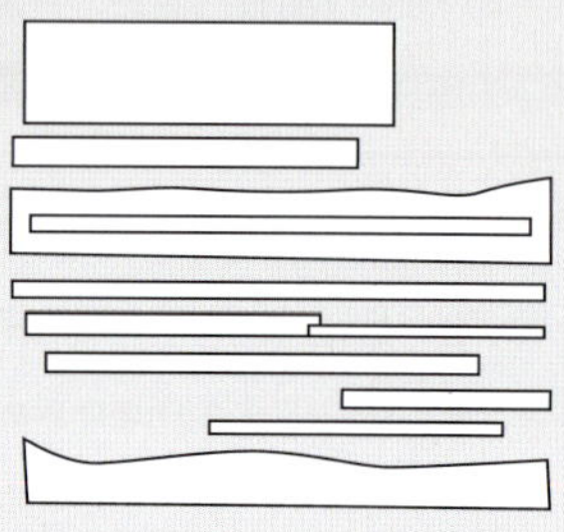

weft

Technique

At this point in your journey, you probably have a stash of paper scraps and strips. Gather strips in varying widths, colors, shapes, and patterns and weave them together.

Materials

- Papers: Assorted strips and pieces

Here you're combining the variety of techniques you've worked on throughout this journey. Different-size strips, different papers, strip weaving, shaped weaving—and with windows to boot! It's a great way to use up papers in your scrap box. The rules are . . . there are no rules.

Instructions

1. Go through your stash and pick out strips and shapes that you like.
2. Weave them together.
3. Glue ends.

Artists' Variations on the Prompt

In this piece, I wove an assortment of paper strips and then cut windows to reveal the variety of papers underneath.

In this totally unstructured weaving, Robin Kessler used a variety of papers left over from the month of weaving.

Weaving 27

Prompt: Modular

The Sum Is Greater Than the Parts

Crafting a piece of art with multiple components creates contrast and depth of field. In my sample weaving for this project, you'll notice three distinct pieces, making it seem as if the bird is flying between day and night. You can create any number of sections in your weaving, but the "rule of odds" in art states that a piece will be more dynamic with an odd number of elements in the composition. For this project, think of three woven modules you can combine. The weaving structures may vary, or they may be similar. Try to make one stand out as the subject.

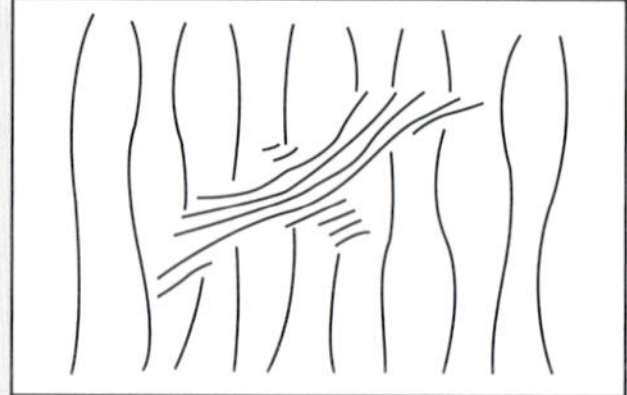

warp

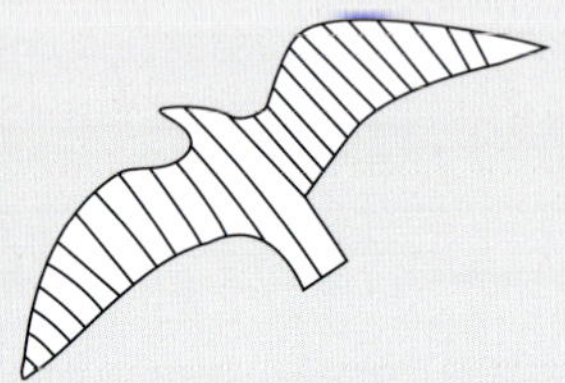

weft #1

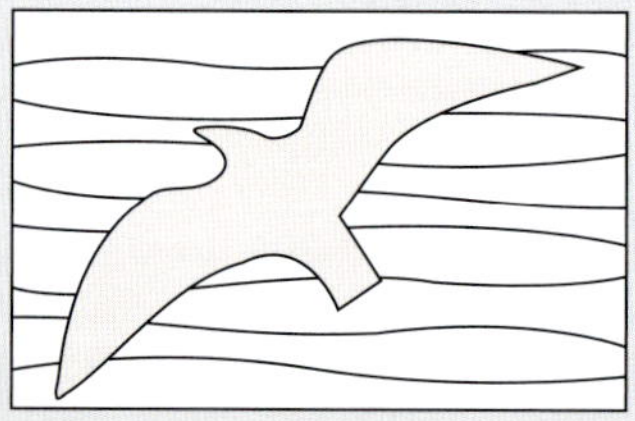

weft #2

Technique

Weave into separate parts of a weaving.

Materials

- Warp paper: 9" × 12" artist-made paper
- Weft papers: Weft #1: 10½" × 7¾" decorative paper (orange with gold fleck); Weft #2: 9" × 12" Thai reversible unryu paper (blue)

Instructions

1. Cut out a bird shape from the orange paper (this is weft piece #1).
2. Trace the shape onto the front of the warp paper.
3. Determine the weaving structure for the shape. Mark the location of the slits inside the bird shape on the warp paper, and then cut them.
4. Cut the orange weft piece into strips, weave them into the warp, carefully erase the pencil marks, and glue the strip ends.
5. Next, trace the woven bird shape onto a sheet of tracing paper.
6. Place the tracing paper on top of weft paper #2 (blue) and cut the shape out in both papers. Cut a ¼" strip from the top and bottom of weft #2 (to compensate for the warp slits not being cut all the way to the edge).
7. Determine the weaving structure for the rest of the weaving. (I pre-sketched my warp slits on a sheet of tracing paper to work around the bird weaving.)

8. Cut slits into the warp—avoid making cuts that run into cuts in the bird.
9. Cut weft #2 into strips and keep them in order. **Note:** A few of the weft strips are cut into two pieces in order to weave around the bird.
10. Start by weaving the central strips that run into the bird to get the strips positioned properly.
11. Carefully glue the weft #2 strip ends on both sides of the paper.
12. Cut windows, as desired. **Note:** I cut windows into the warp (lighter) paper in the upper section to reveal more darkness (sky), and I did the opposite in the lower section to reveal more of the lighter paper to represent Earth.

Artists' Variations on the Prompt

Arlene Brenner wove around a print of one of her own pen-and-ink paintings in two places with two papers to highlight the image. She hand stitched the foliage on the sides.

Susan W. Melczer wove Japanese chiyogami paper into a reproduction of *Echo Park*, 2016, by photographer George Byrne from his 2020 book *Post Truth* for this response to the modular prompt.

(bottom right): The back of Susan's weaving shows the shapes she wove into to create her modular weaving.

Weaving 28

Prompt: Breathe

Give Me Some Space

warp

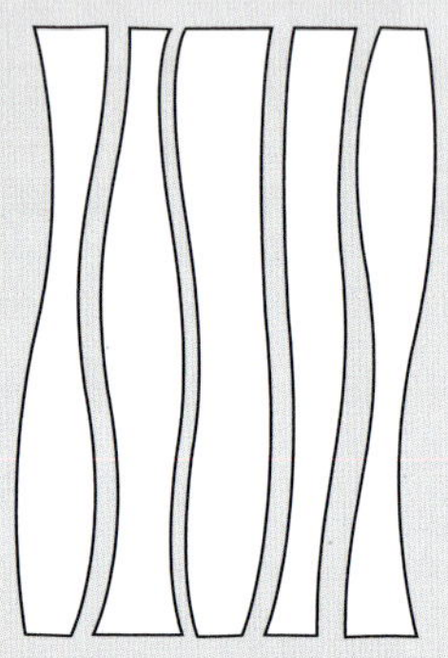

weft

Technique

Spread weft strips apart to allow them to "breathe."

Materials

- Warp paper: 11½" × 11" chiyogami paper
- Weft paper: 14" × 6" artist-made paper

Negative space in artwork leaves room for the viewer's imagination and gives the eyes a break. For this project, you're spreading your weft strips apart so you can let the piece "breathe." How? The weft piece you cut your strips from should be more narrow than the warp so you can spread the strips apart to give them some breathing room.

Instructions

1. Cut a curvy pattern into the top of the warp sheet.
2. Cut the weft sheet into strips approximately 1½" wide.
3. Arrange the weft strips on top of the warp.
4. Carefully cut the warp slits one at a time. (Following the pattern in the paper, I cut short slits the width of each individual weft strip.)
5. Weave the weft strips into the short slits in the warp.
6. Glue the ends.

Artists' Variations on the Prompt

▲ Marguerite Katchen wove artist-made blue and tan papers into a sheet of Mexican amate bark paper (formed with existing gaps) for the breathe prompt and then mounted her weaving on a black paper.

◀ Responding to a prompt to leave space between strips, Patricia Minard wove curved horizontal strips into zigzag slits.

Weaving 29

Prompt: Angle

What's Your Angle?

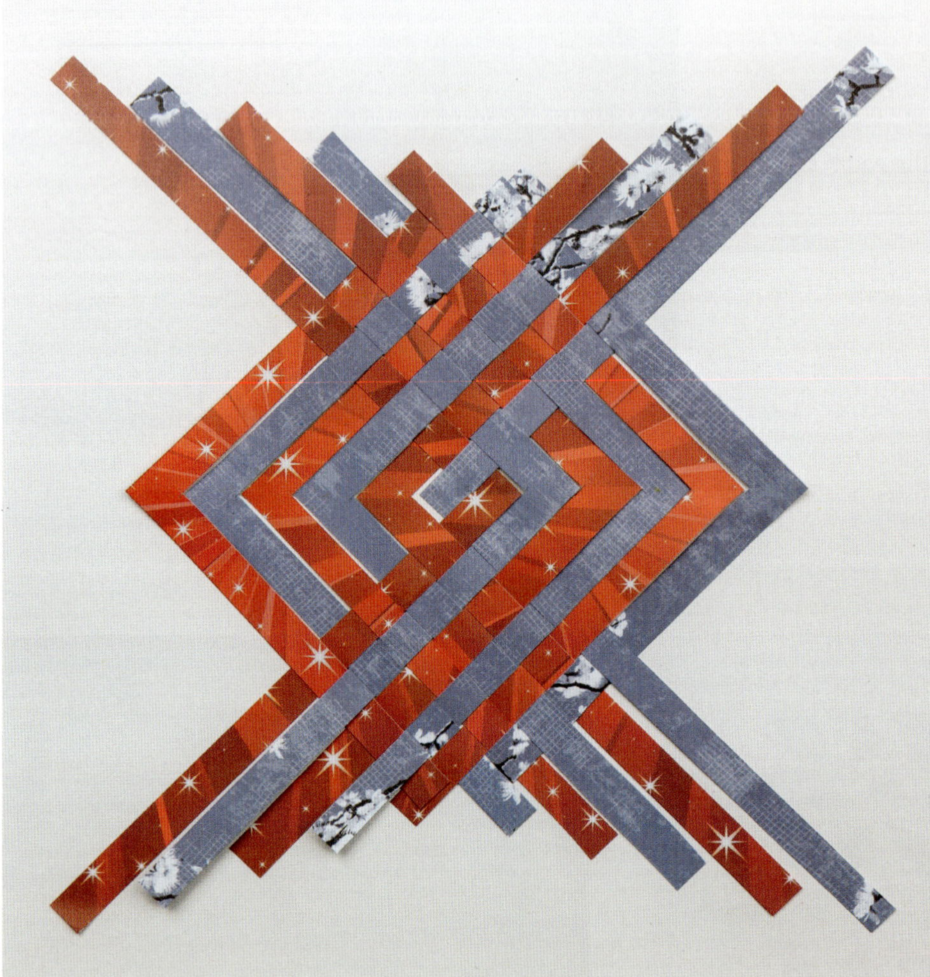

warp

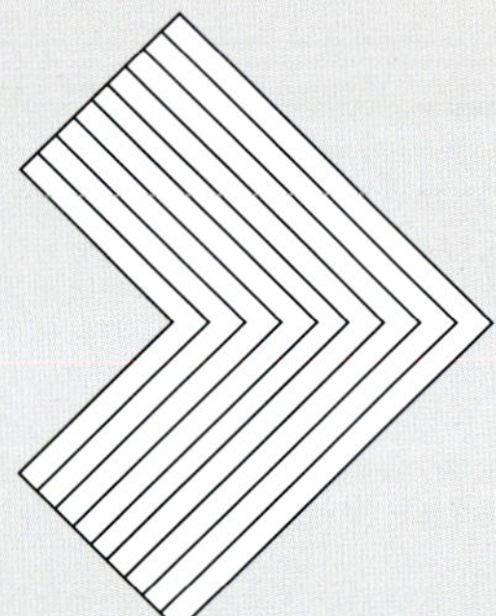

weft

Technique

Cut angled strips.

Materials

- Warp + weft papers: 6" squares of decorative origami papers

Approaching this weaving from a different angle, I used paper cut in 90-degree (right) angles. But you can use smaller (acute) angles or wider (obtuse) angles, or you can even create curved strips. Think of this weaving as intersecting papers at a central point. The visual reminds me of traffic flowing through a busy intersection, or perhaps using overpasses and underpasses. Are your papers solid colors, or does one of them have a pattern? Are there images or features on the ends of the strips, like arrows or symbols? Play with different angles and think about the flow of the lines as you weave.

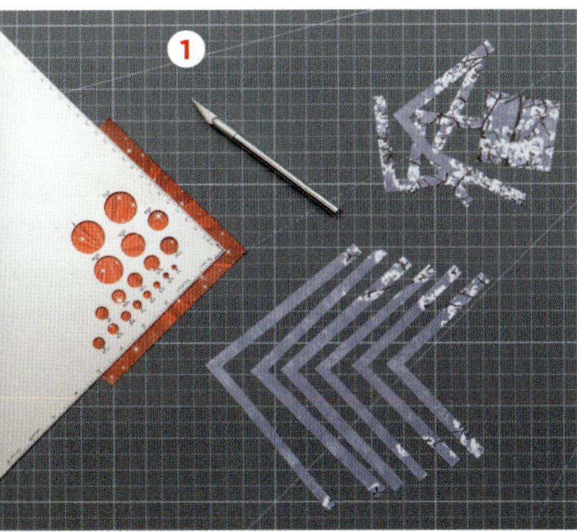

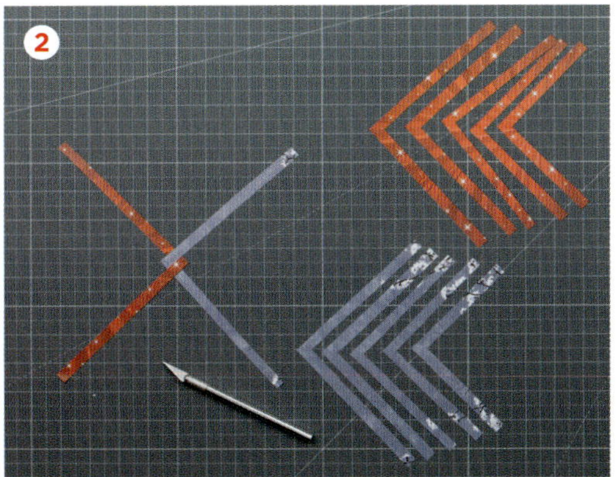

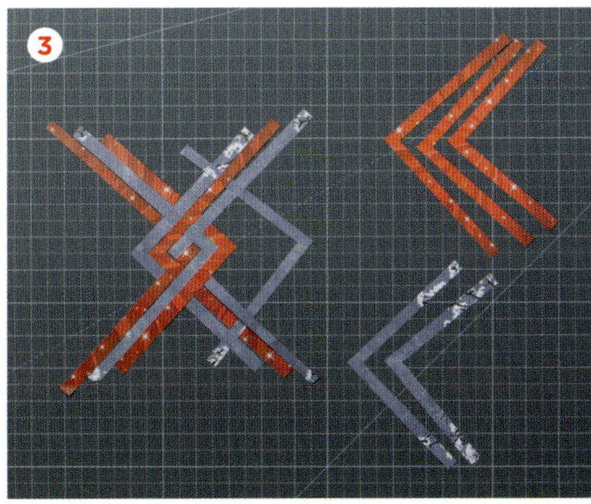

Instructions

1. Refer to the thumbnails as a guide for cutting two sheets of square paper into L-shaped strips.
2. Start with the longest angled strips. Overlap the centers of the two angles, and interlock them, as shown.
3. Weave in the next smallest angles (note that I alternated the colors as I wove).
4. Continue in this fashion until you run out of pieces to weave in.
5. Glue the ends.

Artists' Variations on the Prompt

While kintsugi is usually regarded as a pottery technique, Hilarie Rath works with the concept on paper as a reminder that imperfections are to be honored, as the warp and weft naturally create gaps that let the light shine in. The cracks in pottery or gaps in paper create the need for problem-solving—a flashy background!

I cut strips of Japanese linen papers into curves instead of angles to create this variation.

Weaving 30

Prompt: Puzzle

One Step at a Time

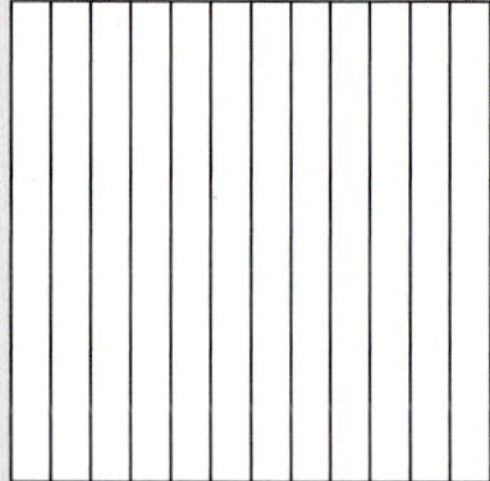

warp

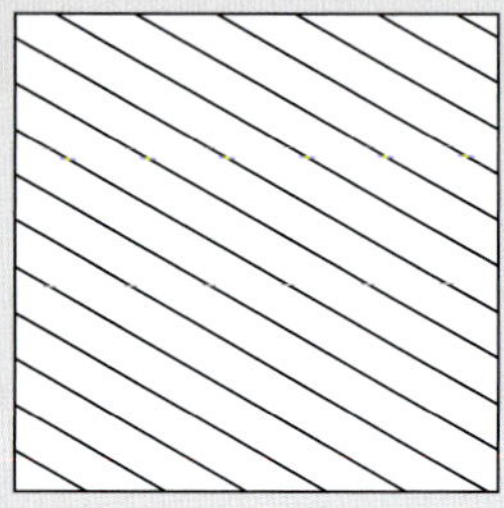

weft #1

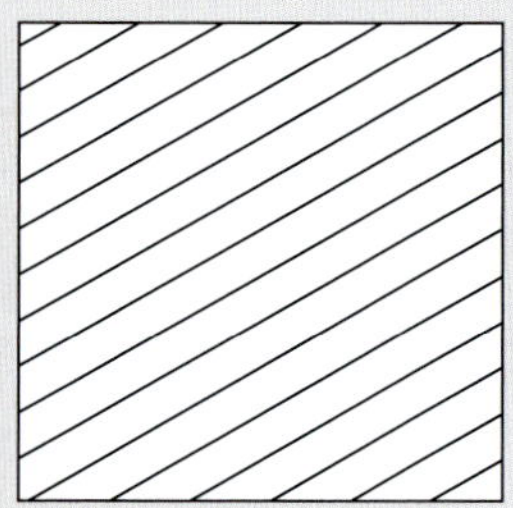

weft #2

Technique

Practice triaxial weaving.

Materials

- Warp paper: 11" × 8½" copier paper
- Weft papers: Two 11" × 8½" sheets in contrasting colors
- Printed downloadable templates (see link on page 210)
- Special tool: Weaving tool (see Resources, page 210)

Now here's a real challenge. But if you're up for it, the result can be wildly rewarding. Tenacity is key—you may have to try a few times before you get it. Don't put too much pressure on yourself and take breaks between steps. Just relax and give it a go . . . or two . . . or three. You will get it, and once you do, you'll be very proud of your accomplishment. It may even become your favorite! For me, mastering the *triaxial* technique was like learning to swim. Once I got it (and it took me several attempts), I could come back to it and, with a quick refresher, dive right in.

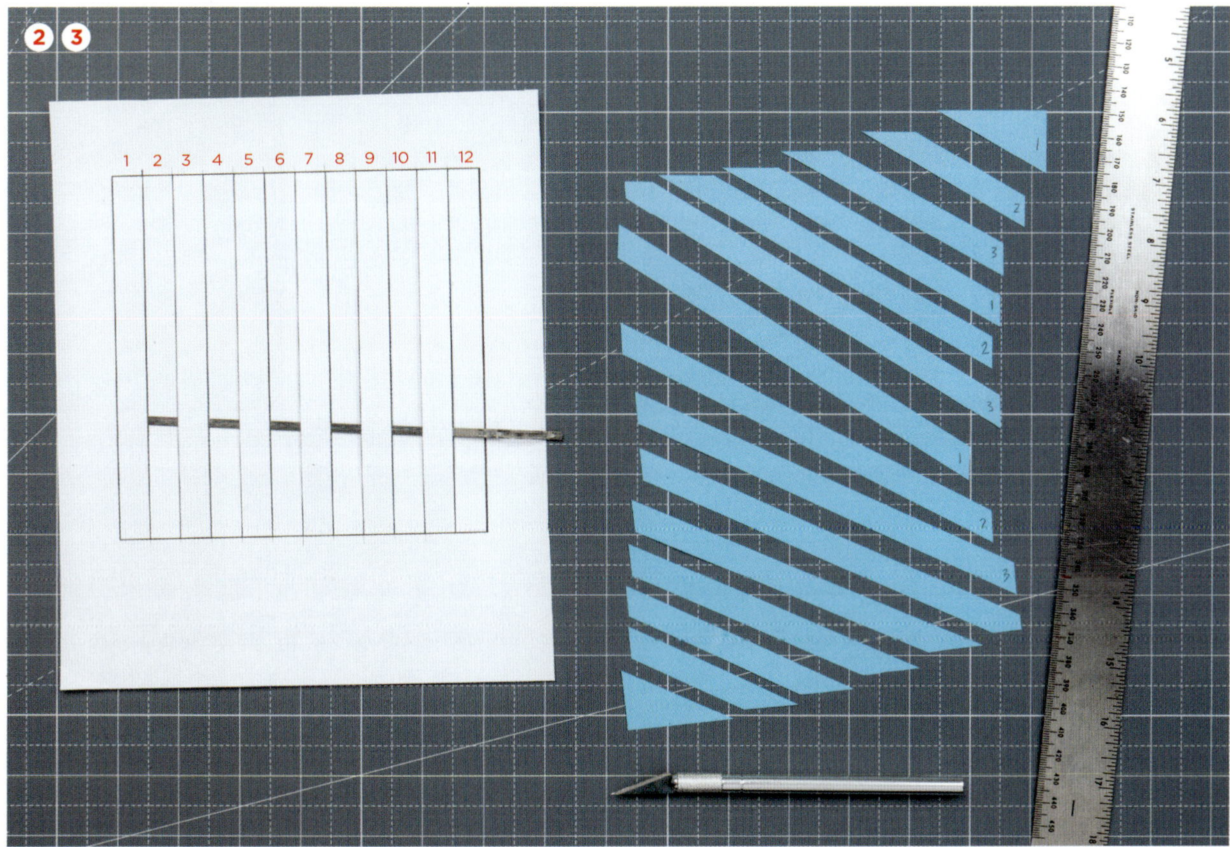

Triaxial weaving goes by many names. The word *triaxial* means, literally, "three axes," and you'll be weaving strips on three axes, which intersect and interlace at 60-degree angles. This type of weaving is also referred to as a "tumbling blocks pattern," which is what it looks like. It has also been called "mad weave," and I can personally attest to the frustration it has caused me—but eventually I mastered it!

Tips

- For your first triaxial weaving, I recommend printing the templates onto the actual papers you will weave—you will need to reference a few things on them.
- I recommend using three solid-colored papers so you can see what is happening on the back side of the weaving.
- Patterned papers look great, but it is best to master this technique before adding additional elements.
- A weaving tool is very helpful in weaving the third set of strips, and it is just the right length for this small triaxial weaving.

Instructions

1. Print the warp and both weft templates onto your papers—I printed the warp template on plain white, weft #1 template on turquoise, and weft #2 template on purple.
2. Warp: Cut along all vertical lines marked on the template, noting that each slit should extend just beyond the outline of the square (at the top and bottom).
3. Weft #1: Cut diagonal strips, following the template, and keep them in order.

The back side of the weaving, with strip 6 woven

The front side of the weaving, with the full set of strips woven

4. The basic weaving structure is over one/under two, and we will establish the pattern with the first three strips. Start in the upper right corner and weave from right to left:
   a. Strip 1 (top right): Over one/under two (I tape this tiny piece in place so that I won't lose it).
   b. Strip 2: Under two/over one/under two.
   c. Strip 3: Under one/over one/under two/over one/under two.
   d. Continue in this pattern. When you get to strip 6, note that it completes the upper left corner of the square. Weave it in.
   e. Flip the weaving over and check the alignment on the back, adjusting as necessary and making sure that the corner of strip 6 is in the right place. You should be able to see the pattern forming on the back and front of your weaving.
   f. Flip the weaving back over and continue weaving.

Note: Once I get about halfway through, I start weaving strips in left to right, because there is more space on the left side of the weaving.

5. Weft #2: Cut the sheet into strips, following the template, and keep them in order.

Note: Weft #2 has longer strips, which simplifies the weaving process (they will be trimmed later). The ends of these strips are rounded, which makes them easier to pull through the layers while weaving.

6. Figuring out where to weave is the trickiest part of getting the second set of strips in, so let's take some time getting set up and studying the structure. The second strips create the three-dimensional tumbling block tops. I recommend that you draw the tops of the blocks on your weaving.
7. Take the strip labeled "start" and place it on top of your weaving, lining up the markings on the right and left sides of the strip with the corresponding sides on the printed warp square.
8. With a pencil, draw two parallel lines along the edges of the strip. Lift the strip and mark the top of each tumbling block—a diamond shape with a slit in the center of each block—with a circle, as shown, on the warp paper. You will mark three tumbling block tops, and these marks will be covered up after the strip is woven in.

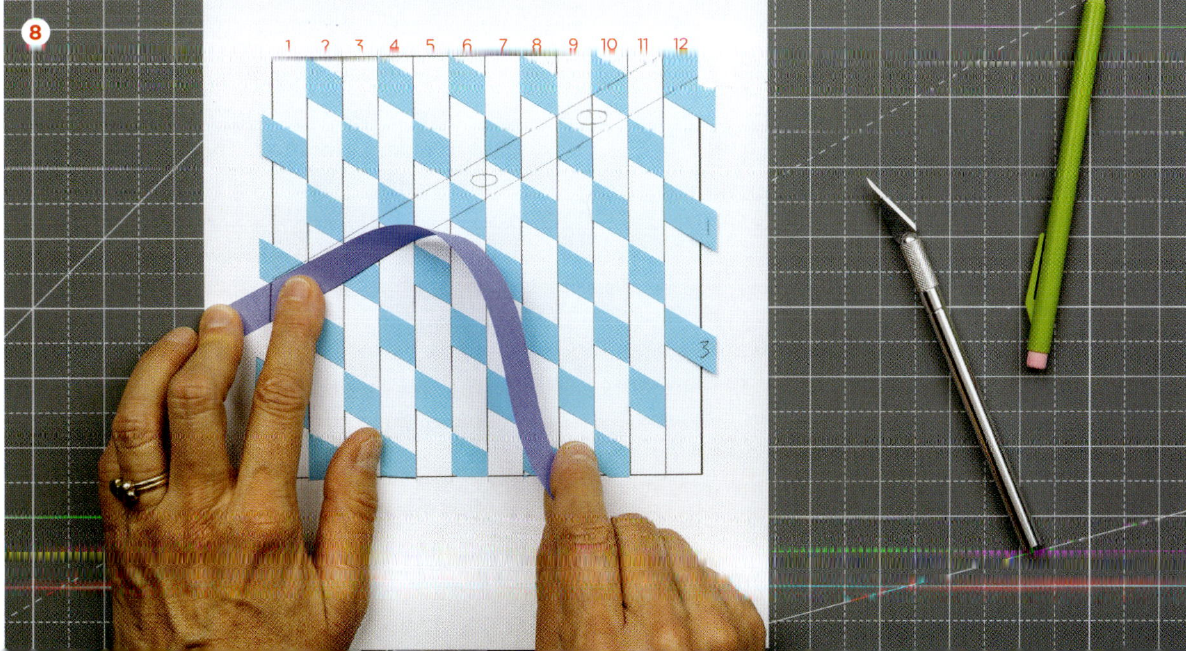

WEAVING IN THE LAST SET OF STRIPS

It is possible to create a triaxial weaving without a weaving tool, but I find that the process is much simpler and quicker with one. You will begin by weaving over the markings you just made.

1. Attach the rounded corner of the unmarked end of the weft strip labeled "start" to the weaving tool. Slip the weaving tool underneath the top blue strip in the upper right-hand corner in column 12, thread it up through the weaving between columns 10 and 11, and pull it over the first tumbling block top. Then thread it back underneath the blue weft strip in column 9.
2. Continue threading the flat end of the weaving tool over and under the double (two-layer) warp so that it lies on top of the box-top markings you made.

Note: The weaving tool needs to slip between the white and blue layers, and you will have to pay attention to get it between the layers correctly in order to cover your markings. Once you do this a few times, you'll get the hang of it.

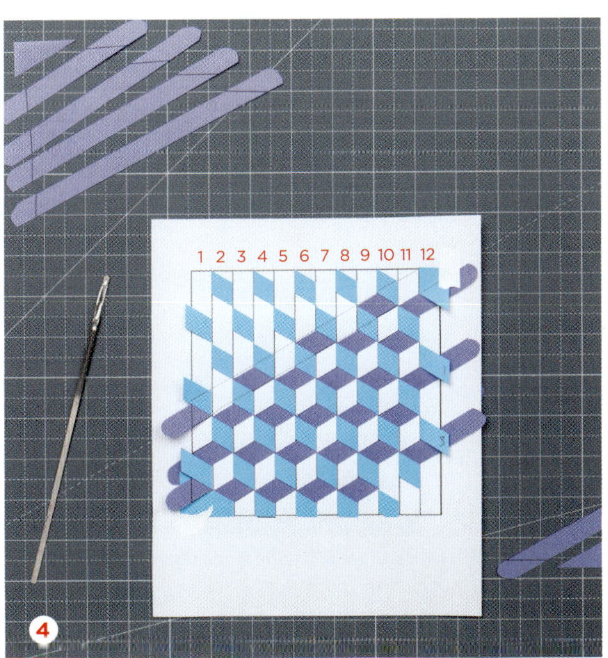

The finished weaving

3. Carefully pull the strip all the way through the weaving as shown. Release the weaving tool. You've woven your first strip!
4. Mark the next set of tumbling blocks, if desired. Continue weaving in this pattern until all strips are woven in.

TO FINISH

1. Tighten up your weaving, if necessary, and then carefully trim the edges around the perimeter.
2. Check to make sure you have the edge pieces woven correctly and glue the ends.

Congratulations! You have completed a complex puzzle.

Artists' Variations on the Prompt

▲ Beverly Frey was inspired by a basket-weaving pattern and created her own strips with a color pattern: first strip set, white/white/blue; second strip set, white/white/green; third strip set, white/white/red.

◀ Davida Feder used three copies of a photograph she took for this weaving. She made slight adjustments for saturation and brightness to the copies in Photoshop to enhance the pattern.

More Triaxial Tips

If you're interested in learning more about triaxial weaving, check out Shereen LaPlantz's *The Mad Weave Book* (see Suggested Reading, page 211). It focuses on basket weaving, but her weaving structures can be translated into paper. LaPlantz was an internationally recognized book artist, basket weaver, and author who passed away too young. She also wrote other books about basketry and bookmaking. I have a hunch that she may have been the first to use paper strips in basketry.

◀ Gina Pisello's variation on the triaxial weave is done by using a pattern of two dark strips and one light strip repeated across each of the three sides. The tricky part of this pattern was getting the light-colored strips in the right places to form the diamonds that highlight the stars.

▶ After mastering the difficult triaxial weave, Therese Lennert couldn't get enough of it, finding the regularity and geometry so interesting to the eye. Here she combines uniform monochrome papers with a textured and colored monotype.

6 WEAVING PROJECTS TO SHOWCASE YOUR WORK

Weavings don't have to be two-dimensional. Here are a few projects to showcase your weaving prowess. Integrate a small weaving onto a note card, create an album to store your weavings, and sculpt a woven paper lantern to highlight the windows cut into the layers.

We all have our own life to pursue, our own kind of dream to be weaving, and we all have the power to make wishes come true, as long as we keep believing.

—Louisa May Alcott, American novelist and author of *Little Women*

Woven Note Card

Materials

- Warp paper: 10" × 7" light cardstock, grain short (see Grain Direction, below)
- Weft paper: 6" × 4" decorative paper

Create your own one-of-a-kind note card. In this project you'll weave a decorative paper into the front of a note card. Vary the paper you choose for the mood of the occasion.

Grain Direction

Paper has a grain, just as wood does. Grain direction is particularly important when the paper is being folded. When manufactured commercially, paper fibers align in the direction of flow on the machine. When you buy sheets of paper, you purchase sheets that have been cut down from larger sheets or rolls. In general, the longer dimension indicates the grain direction (for example, the grain on a 22" × 40" sheet runs in the 40" direction). For this project, you'll want the grain of the cardstock running in the 7" direction, so that the card folds in half easily.

Instructions

1. Fold the cardstock (warp sheet) in half and place the decorative weft paper on what will become the back side (inside) of the front of the card. Center the weft sheet within the 7" × 5" space and trace the outline.
2. For the warp: Cut vertical curved slits, starting just above the top pencil line. Space them approximately 1" apart, ending slightly below the bottom pencil line.
3. For the weft: Cut horizontal curved strips that are approximately 1" wide.
4. Weave the weft strips into the warp, one at a time, using the pencil lines on the back as a guide for placing strips.
5. Erase the pencil marks.
6. Glue ends on both sides.
7. Optional: Cut windows.

Note: My paper has a pattern on both sides, and I wove on the back/inside of the card so that I could see the guidelines as I wove.

Reverse Piano Hinge Album

This album creates a lovely storage space for your weavings. As far as I can tell, the structure originated in Australia. I discovered it in a blog post, and the binding also appears in Gwen Diehn's book *Live & Learn: Real Life Journals: Designing & Using Handmade Books*. She calls it a flat-style Australian reverse piano hinge. I shortened the name and added a few twists.

Materials

- 6 book pages: cover-weight paper (at least 80 lb) cut to 8¼" × 16½", grain short (see Grain Direction, page 176)
- 6 spine inserts: Sturdy cardstock (I used the same paper as the book pages) cut to ⅝" × 8¼"; adjust width as needed
- Tyvek or another spine paper that folds well and doesn't tear easily, cut to 11" × 6", grain short
- Glue + brush or double-sided tape
- Scoring board, bone folder, or scoring tool

Note:
Tyvek is a strong, paperlike material that some mailing envelopes are made of—you might even recycle one for this project. It is easy to stain with acrylic paint, which brings out the fibrous texture—simply rub paint into the surface with a sponge.

PAPER ATTRIBUTES

You can make this book any size with any number of pages. I recommend a fairly stiff paper for the pages and a light to midweight paper for the spine—it will accordion-fold several times, so make sure it folds well.

Instructions

1. Score the book pages: Measure and mark the center of each book page and score along the centerfold of each folio so that they fold into 8¼" square folios.
2. Mark the endpoints for a slit on the spine of each book page, 1" from the top and bottom edges.
3. Cut a vertical slit along the spine of each book page between your marks.

4. Accordion-fold your Tyvek spine paper into 14 sections as follows:
   a. Fold the paper in half, short side to short side, and crease it well. Reinforce the fold with a bone folder if you have one.
   b. Open the paper and place the peak of the mountain fold you just made face up, then align it with one cut edge. Crease the new folded edge.
   c. Fold over the remaining cut edge, aligning it with the other sections. Crease the new fold. This makes a 4-section accordion.
   d. Reverse the center valley fold into a mountain fold. You now have three mountain folds.

4e

4f

4g

4h

e. Align the peak of the topmost mountain fold with the nearest cut edge. Crease the new folded edge.

f. Repeat with the remaining folds, stacking each fold on top of the previous fold. Fold over the final cut edge, lining it up with the folded edge. Crease well. Unfold to reveal an 8-section accordion.

g. Flip the paper over and reverse all valley folds into mountain folds.

h. *Do not* fold the first and last sections this time, but fold all the other sections in half again. You will end up with two wider sections on the ends and 12 skinnier sections between them.

5

6

8

9

5. Slip one of the wider single-layer ends of the accordion-folded Tyvek spine into the slit in the back cover. Leave it in place and close the folio (you will attach this piece in step 8).
6. Insert the spine pieces: Set the next folio on top, open it, and thread the first accordion-folded section into the slit. Slip a spine insert into the accordion-folded section to lock the page in place. (Note that the spine inserts are the same height as the book pages, extending beyond the top and bottom of the accordion-folded sections.) Adjust the width of the spine pieces, if necessary—they should be snug.
7. Continue adding pages to the book by tucking subsequent accordion-folded sections into the folio slits and slipping spine inserts into sleeves.
8. Once you have inserted the Tyvek between all of the pages and inserted the spine pieces, slip the single layer of Tyvek between the inside front cover and the first page. Apply double-sided tape to the Tyvek, as shown, and affix it to the first page. Affix the other end of the Tyvek (seen in Step 5) to the last page.
9. Attach artwork to pages with double-sided tape or any other method you choose (e.g., photo corners, glue dots, stitching).

Optional: I laminated the front cover to the page behind it with sheet adhesive, trapping the spine piece between the two to create a sturdy cover. I laminated the back cover in the same fashion. You can adorn the cover by adhering another weaving.

Artist Variation on Reverse Piano Hinge Album

▲ Kristi Galbraith cut large windows through both layers of her folios to display both sides of her interpretation of various Froebel-style paper weavings. ►

Woven Paper Lantern

Get sculptural! Make a flat weaving, bring it into the round, connect the ends with a unique woven hinge, and illuminate it.

PAPER ATTRIBUTES

At least one of the papers should be translucent to allow light through when illuminated, and one of the papers (either one) should be a light cardstock weight to give your lantern some rigidity.

Materials

- Warp paper, cut to 6" × 11", grain short (see Grain Direction, page 176)
- Weft paper, cut to 5" × 8¾", grain short
- One bamboo skewer, ⅛" diameter and at least 6" long
- White glue
- Hinge template printed on cardstock (see link on page 210)
- Battery-operated tea light
- Heavy-duty scissors or garden clippers

Instructions

1. Score and fold in the two ends of the larger paper (the warp) at 1⁄2". Note that the smaller paper should fit lengthwise between the two folded ends.
2. Center the smaller piece of paper (the weft) on the warp and note that there is a 1⁄2" margin at the top and bottom of the warp. Remove the weft paper and cut a series of wavy vertical lines between those invisible 1⁄2" margins (the margins do not need to be exact, but make sure that you do not cut all the way to either edge). I cut seven slits that are about 1" apart.
3. Cut the weft paper into four or five wavy horizontal strips.

4

6

4. Place the warp on your work surface with the folded ends tucked under. Keeping the weft strips in order, weave them into the warp one at a time. Alternate the over/under pattern strip by strip. If the last strip is too wide, trim the straight side to make it easier to weave (see Working the Last Strip, page 45).

5. Carefully glue down any loose ends on both sides of the weaving.

6. Place a mini cutting mat between the woven paper sections and cut windows. I usually cut into the opaque paper, but you could cut windows into the translucent sheet instead, or you can cut windows in both papers.

THE HINGE

1. Cut out the hinge template and place it on top of one of the folded ends of the lantern. Cut small triangles through both layers of the folded hinge. Flip the template over and cut the same triangular slots on the opposite folded edge.
2. Use a straightedge and bone folder to score every other tab on one hinge. Repeat on the other side of the lantern, scoring and folding the alternating tabs.
3. Fold the scored, alternating tabs back and forth and then tuck them inside, as shown.
4. Carefully apply glue to the edge of the hinge (take care not to get glue into the space where the skewer will go). Also apply glue to the bottom edges of the vertical "stair steps" on the tucked tabs, as shown. Apply pressure to glue the hinges in place. Repeat on the other side.
5. Thread the skewer through alternating hinges and trim the skewer ends. Grab a tea light and illuminate your lantern!

7 GALLERY

The following pages are filled with a sampling of weavings by contemporary artists who incorporate paper weaving into their practice. These works are as varied as their materials, ranging from found posters to discarded library items to two- and three-dimensional works of art.

The continuous repetitive action of weaving is similar to reading and reciting, implying that, through the repetition of a task or ritual, one has the possibility to transcend the mundane.

—**Carole Kunstadt**, artist

◄ Detail of front cover weaving by Helen Hiebert

Hollie Chastain
Telling Stories Through Weaving

Hollie Chastain is a mixed-media artist and illustrator who works in Chattanooga, Tennessee. Coming from both a graphic design and studio art background, her aesthetic has a storytelling quality—a mix of found material, strong graphic elements, and modern palettes—that she has applied to a wide range of illustration and editorial work. Hollie teaches workshops across the United States and maintains a home studio, where she creates commissioned pieces for clients around the world.

Hollie points out, "I started weaving with intent at the beginning of a long winter in 2018. I had just finished up a big show that consisted of a collection of smaller minimal pieces with clippings and color blocking. Although I had woven paper before, it was never with the intention of working it into a complete mixed-media piece. My current work combines paper weaving, collage, and mixed media."

Psychopomp I, by Hollie Chastain, 2018. 6" × 6", paper, thread.

Psychopomp III, by Hollie Chastain, 2019. 7" × 7", paper.

Psychopomp II, by Hollie Chastain, 2018. 6" × 6", paper, thread.

Galen Gibson-Cornell
Urban Explorer

Galen Gibson-Cornell was born and raised in Maryville, Missouri, and received a bachelor of fine arts degree in printmaking from Truman State University, Kirksville, Missouri, in 2009 (his time there included a year of studying abroad in Angers, France). He completed a master of fine arts degree at the University of Wisconsin in 2013 and set off on a yearlong Fulbright fellowship to Budapest, Hungary. In the following years, Galen traveled to multiple international artist-residency programs, developing a creative practice based on urban exploration and repurposing found materials. His studio has been based in Philadelphia since 2017.

Says Galen, "I am fascinated with once-functional materials, specifically street posters. An itinerant traveler, I explore cities on foot, studying the layers of 'urban skin'—posters, flyers, and paper advertisements that cover walls and signboards. My practice combines urban exploration, repurposing found materials, and principles of détournement (meaning 'diversion,' which is quite different than the meaning of the original street posters)."

Queen, by Galen Gibson-Cornell, 2022. 53" × 59", found street posters from Sofia, Bulgaria, sliced and woven.

Montagne Flambée (*Flaming Mountain*), by Galen Gibson-Cornell, 2022. 60" × 40" × 4", found street posters from New York City, sliced and woven.

▲ *Aerial*, by Galen Gibson-Cornell, 2022. 78″ × 110″, found street posters from Berlin, Germany; Plovdiv and Sofia, Bulgaria; Buenos Aires, Argentina; New York City and Philadelphia; Venice, Italy; sliced and woven.

◄ Galen Gibson-Cornell in his Philadelphia studio

Aerial, by Galen Gibson-Cornell, 2022 (detail; see page 193)

Naomi J. Kendall
Pushing the Possibilities of Paper

Naomi J. Kendall is an artist based in Somerset in the UK. She completed a foundation course at Cheltenham School of Art and pursued a degree in art history from Leicester University and a postgraduate degree in gallery and museum studies from Manchester University. After a career working in galleries, in community arts, and as director of an arts charity in London, she returned to making her own work in 2011. Naomi exhibits her work internationally and is featured as a master artisan in the Michelangelo Foundation's Homo Faber Guide, an online platform dedicated to craftsmanship that allows you to discover artisans and their masterpieces, explore museums, visit galleries and shops selling one-of-a-kind objects, and enjoy artistic experiences in cities across Europe.

Naomi notes, "I describe my work as woven paper, but it also includes folding and layering. I love working in color, but I also create monochrome work, sometimes adding marks or textures with pencil, ink, and paint. I set out to push the possibilities of working with paper to create pieces of artwork that surprise and puzzle the viewer. I sketch and take photographs when I am traveling or just out in the world, where I discover patterns in fragments of buildings or street architecture. I love exploring textiles, woven objects, and colorful ceramics in museum collections. I keep many sketchbooks, and one is always dedicated to recording color combinations I see as I go about my life."

Binca Blue, by Naomi J. Kendall, 2023. Approximately 16½" × 11¾", woven paper. This work is part of a series of pieces inspired by the colors of Welsh tapestry blankets and, for Naomi, reminiscent of the process of embroidering on Binca fabric as a child.

Strata, by Naomi J. Kendall, 2021. Approximately 29½" × 27½", woven paper. This is an architectural piece, inspired by light and shade playing on buildings. Naomi used to live in Barcelona with a view of balconies and canopies from her apartment, and the city continues to influence her work.

Latitude, by Naomi J. Kendall, 2021. Approximately 21¾" × 20¾", woven paper. *Latitude* was made as part of a collaborative project with other paper artists who each made a piece representing a month of the year for a charity calendar. Naomi's piece represents November, or autumn around the world, and each color is unique.

Carole Kunstadt
Weaving Memory and History

Following her graduation from Hartford Art School in West Hartford, Connecticut, and postgraduate studies at the Akademie der Bildenden Künste in Munich, Germany, Carole Kunstadt was an apprentice and then an assistant at a tapestry workshop in New York City, where she wove large-scale photo-realism tapestries for corporations. Her own woven pieces began by working with pages from an antique book of psalms, intuitively cutting the paper into strips and weaving them together. Through the exploration of materials—antique books, bookplates, music manuscripts, and artifacts—history, memory, and time merge in a hybrid form.

Carole explains, "In my Sacred Poem Series, pages of psalms and hymns, dating from 1844 to 1849, are cut and recombined, resulting in a presentation that evokes an ecumenical offering—poems of praise and gratitude. Visually, there is a consistent and measured cadence to a page of psalms, which is echoed in the reductive and additive process of weaving the paper. The fragmented text suggests the temporal quality of our lives and the vulnerability of memory and history. The continuous repetitive action of weaving is similar to reading and reciting, implying that, through the repetition of a task or ritual, one has the possibility to transcend the mundane."

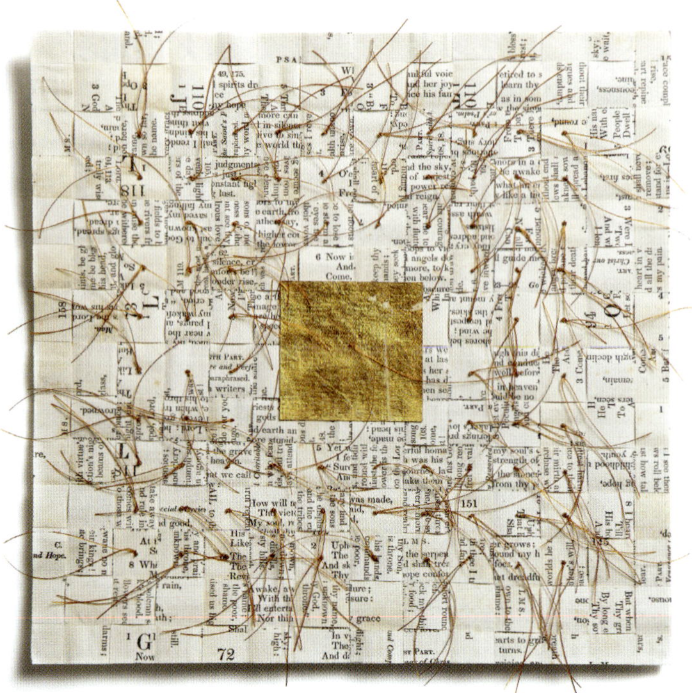

Sacred Poem LXVII, by Carole Kunstadt, 2010. 9" × 9", nylon thread, gold leaf, paper—pages from *Parish Psalmody,* dated 1849 (504 knots). Photo by Kevin Kunstadt.

Sacred Poem LXXXIX, by Carole Kunstadt, 2014. 5" × 6½" × 2½", 24-karat gold leaf, interfacing, paper—pages from *Parish Psalmody,* dated 1849.

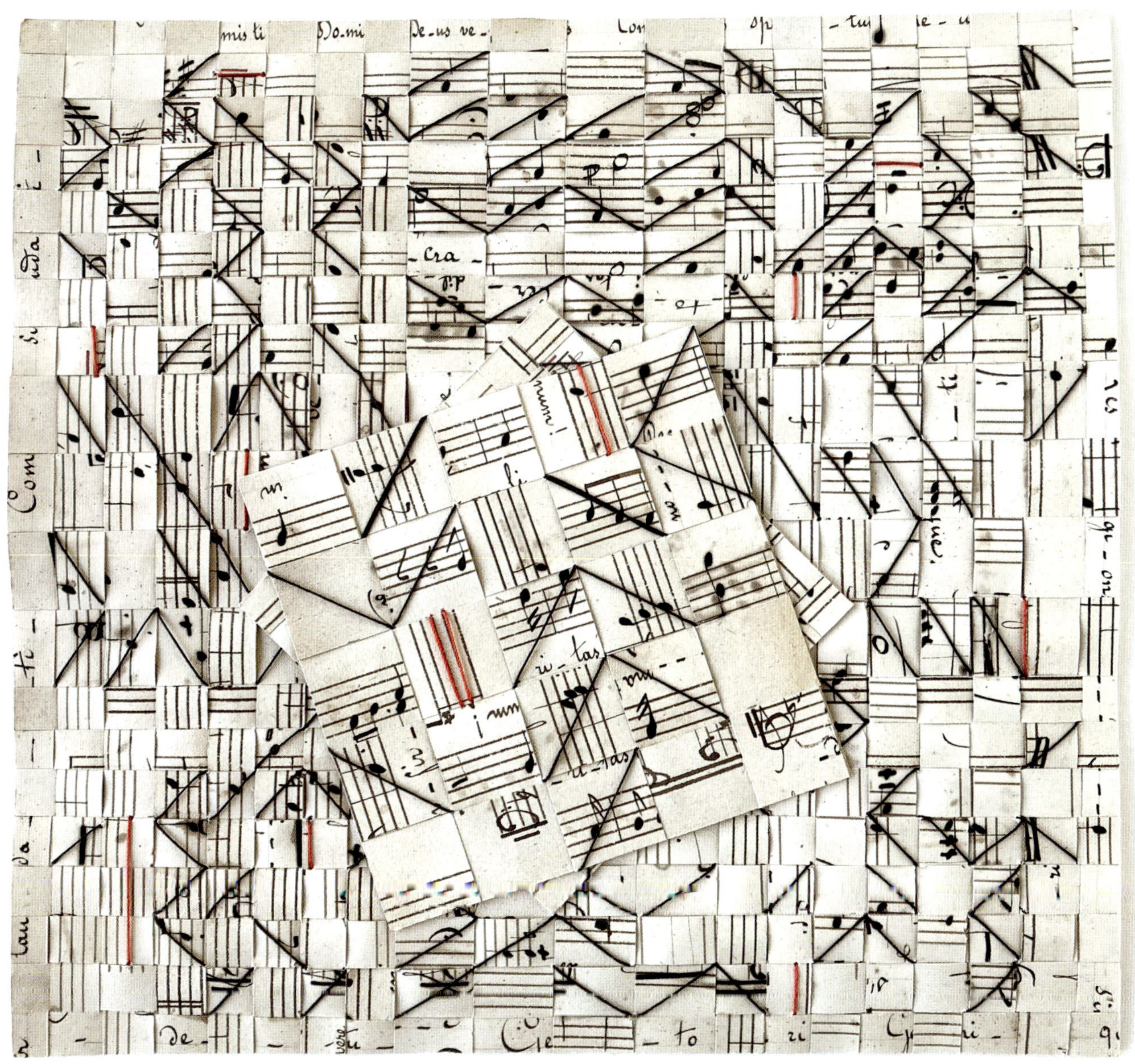

Interlude No. 23, by Carole Kunstadt, 2021. 8¼" × 8½", thread, oak gall ink on paper—nineteenth-century music manuscripts published by Dantier/Paris. This weaving remixes hand-cut nineteenth-century music manuscripts, responding to the existing marks and their graphic patterns and recombining them.

Dorothy McGuinness
Master of Diagonal Twill

Dorothy McGuinness lives and works in Everett, Washington. She took her first basketmaking class in 1987 and has studied basket-weaving techniques that have been handed down through the centuries. Dorothy has worked extensively with Jiro Yonezawa, a contemporary Japanese basket maker and teacher. She discovered her medium of choice in 2000, when she took a workshop with Jackie Abrams, who introduced her to watercolor paper as a basket-weaving material. She now works exclusively in diagonal twills and mad weave, creating contemporary sculptural baskets, and enjoys exploring the interplay of weaving, color, and design in her sculptural woven paper pieces. Dorothy is the author of *The Art of Contemporary Woven Paper Basketry* (see Suggested Reading, page 211).

Dorothy observes, "After years of exploring the woven form, I mastered the art of diagonal twill, which I use to create forms and structures not normally found in basketry. My medium for this unique work is watercolor paper, which I hand-paint and cut into uniform strips. Approaching my work as a puzzle drives me to discover new shapes and come up with weaving innovations. I am interested in math and geometric constraints and am intrigued by the potential outcome of any new design. The evolution of my body of work is built on taking risks and avoiding the 'known.' The risks offer challenges, which often lead to new directions. This is the excitement that keeps me working in a repetitive medium."

Shooting Stars, by Dorothy McGuinness, 2019. 9" × 12" × 10", watercolor paper, acrylic paint, waxed linen thread. This piece is done in mad weave, using three separate starts to weave the piece.

Byzantine, by Dorothy McGuinness, 2019. 9" × 20" × 14", watercolor paper, acrylic paint, polyester thread. This piece is done in mad weave. It was woven in a long strip that was then twisted and woven together to create the Möbius form. The paper had to be precisely painted to get the two sets of tumbling blocks motifs to line up at the overlap.

Variation on a Theme 4, by Dorothy McGuinness, 2022. 8" × 14" × 9", watercolor paper, acrylic paint, waxed linen thread. This piece is part of a series in which each basket starts with a base using a different number of weavers.

Rhiannon "Skye" Tafoya
Celebrating Cherokee and Santa Clara Pueblo Weaving Traditions

Rhiannon "Skye" Tafoya (Eastern Band of Cherokee and Santa Clara Pueblo) employs printmaking, digital design, and basketry techniques in creating her artist's books, prints, and paper weavings. Both of her tribal heritages, cultures, and lineages are manifested in her two- and three-dimensional artworks, which range in size from a few inches to a few feet. She is inspired by her family history of basketry and observing her father and maternal grandmother weave baskets from red willow, honeysuckle vines, and white oak. While her inspiration comes, in part, from Cherokee traditions, her artworks are decidedly contemporary, featuring sharp lines and bold colors. Skye creates with an intention of combating erasure by sharing personal and familial stories and her own cultural learnings, along with her own usage of the Cherokee language.

Skye recalls, "I used to gather red willow and weave willow baskets with my father during the winter, and some of my earliest memories of my maternal grandmother are watching her naturally dye and weave baskets out of honeysuckle vines and white oak. I owe my art practice to these loving memories. Paper weaving is my way of keeping my loved ones and ancestors close when they're not physically present; a way to keep them informed about my life; and a way to describe my personal lifestyle. I am fascinated with the knowledge, the effort, and the caretaking involved in basketmaking, both in the gathering and in the weaving processes. I think it resembles variations of the processes within bookmaking and printmaking, which is why I continuously choose to work in these mediums. I notice and appreciate how each step informs the next and that thinking backward is essential to understanding the outcome. I also treat my visits to printmaking studios (as a visiting artist) as a 'gathering process' for materials, where I print papers that I use in my weavings. My relationship to the basket, my culture, my language, and my personal and family narratives are influential to the art that I create, whether it be a digital design, a paper weaving, a print, or a book. My creative work is a way to preserve and share narratives that otherwise would be left out of the dialogue."

Contraction, by Rhiannon "Skye" Tafoya, 2021. 15¾" × 17", Colorplan papers. *Contraction* is about the 60-plus hours of labor the artist endured before having an emergency C-section. The center of the weaving shows Skye's uterus, and the pattern surrounding the center represents the movement of her uterus during each contraction.

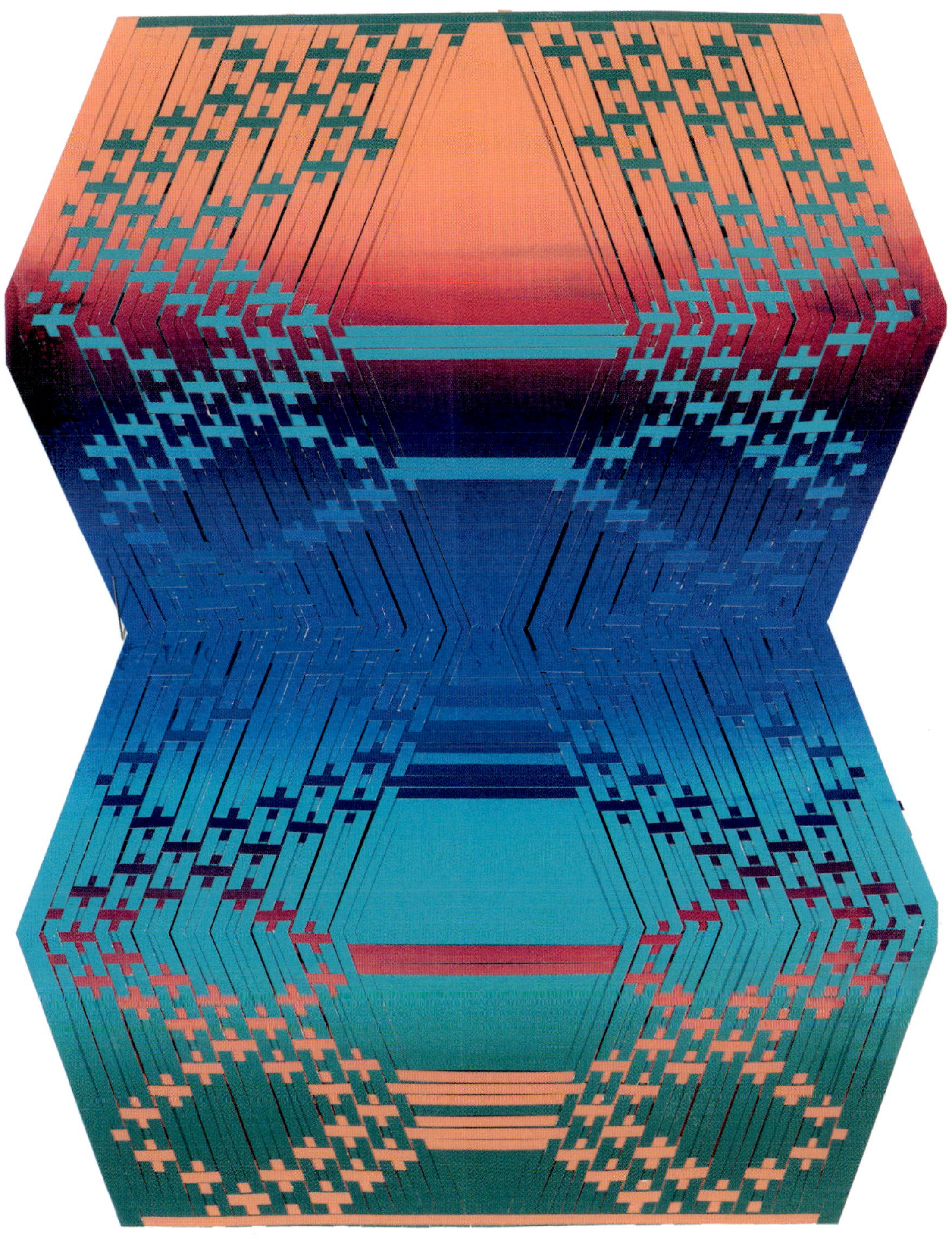

Rhythmic, by Rhiannon "Skye" Tafoya, 2021. 14" × 11", screen print woven with a screen print. Skye's 60-plus-hour labor and birth were a painful and scary experience. Before deciding to get an epidural after 59 hours, she was continuously in a meditation to keep her mind steady through the laboring pain. *Rhythmic* represents the meditation that helped her endure the intense labor and life-threatening birth.

Julie VonDerVellen
Reimagining the Book

Julie VonDerVellen is an artist and design educator. She received her bachelor of science degree in graphic design from Edgewood College in Madison, Wisconsin, and her master of fine arts at the University of Wisconsin–Madison. She is an assistant professor of graphic design at Carroll University in Waukesha, Wisconsin. Julie has exhibited widely, and her artist books are in special collections at university libraries around the United States.

"My work redefines the traditional book structure while narrating the union between emotion and memorization," Julie points out. "Sculptures, collages, and paintings document the landscapes, successes, and some tribulations I have encountered throughout my personal journey. Piece by piece, handmade paper and book-related artifacts unravel into ⅛" strips and then transition back into a woven form with the help of a sewing needle. As the fibers warp and weft, pixel-like patterns emerge, exposing the influences of beauty and the complexities found in nature, my profession, and relationships."

Bright Side, by Julie VonDerVellen, 2022. 8½" × 8½", artist-made paper, watercolor. This piece is inspired by the vivid, awakening pastel colors of Wisconsin's spring and summer seasons and a correlating uplifted state of mind.

Date Due: Withdrawn, by Julie VonDerVellen, 2022. 6¼" × 12½", artist-made paper, recycled library date-due cards. This piece was made with ⅛" strips of Korean hanji artist-made paper and recycled date-due cards from Carroll University's library. This weaving is a historical snapshot of the educational experience—student learning, faculty research, and librarian contributions—at the institution. Date cards like these are rare now, and the weaving captures the nostalgic experience of having a book physically stamped during the checkout process. Many of the date stamps within this piece correlate with the midterm and final exam schedules in October, December, March, and May.

Checking In, by Julie VonDerVellen, 2022. 11½" × 7⅛", artist-made paper, acrylic. This piece was inspired by antique textiles and fabric swatch books, and the ¼" and 1/16" strips weave through the light pink Korean hanji paper.

Therese Zemlin
Weaving Poetry and Photography

Therese Zemlin has worked in a range of media, including paper, welded steel, light, digital media, and natural materials. Her work ranges from small sculpture to large installations and is inspired by elements and phenomena of the ever-changing natural world. She has exhibited her work nationally and has received numerous grants. After earning a BFA from the University of Illinois at Urbana-Champaign and an MFA from the University of Texas at Austin, Therese taught fibers and sculpture at the University of South Carolina in Columbia; Appalachian State University in Boone, North Carolina; and Phillips Academy in Andover, Massachusetts. She currently divides her time between St. Paul and the Northwoods of Minnesota.

"Interlacing has been a recurring theme in my work, manifesting as layered cut paper, painted and drawn pattern, and tetrahedral twig structures hanging by threads from the ceiling," Therese explains. "In 2020, due to the pandemic, I was faced with developing projects that students could do at home with whatever they could scrounge, so I started experimenting with homemade cardboard looms, using household string for warp and strips of fabric, plastic, foil, and paper for weft. This led to a woven poetry assignment using strips of found text as weft. While weaving sample works for the assignments, I realized the potential for my own studio work. The bringing together of photo-based inkjet prints; strips of text from Rachel Carson, John Muir, and various philosophers; and the collection of historic and contemporary weaving drafts, so generously made available on Handweaving.net, has resulted in a way of working and thinking that is familiar terrain, while also introducing text and woven structure as physical components of the work."

The Last Drop: Rocks and Water, by Therese Zemlin, 2021. 11" × 13", inkjet prints on Japanese paper, book pages; weaving draft by Ivo Kastanak, Austria, 1903, from Handweaving.net. Book pages from Rachel Carson's *Silent Spring*.

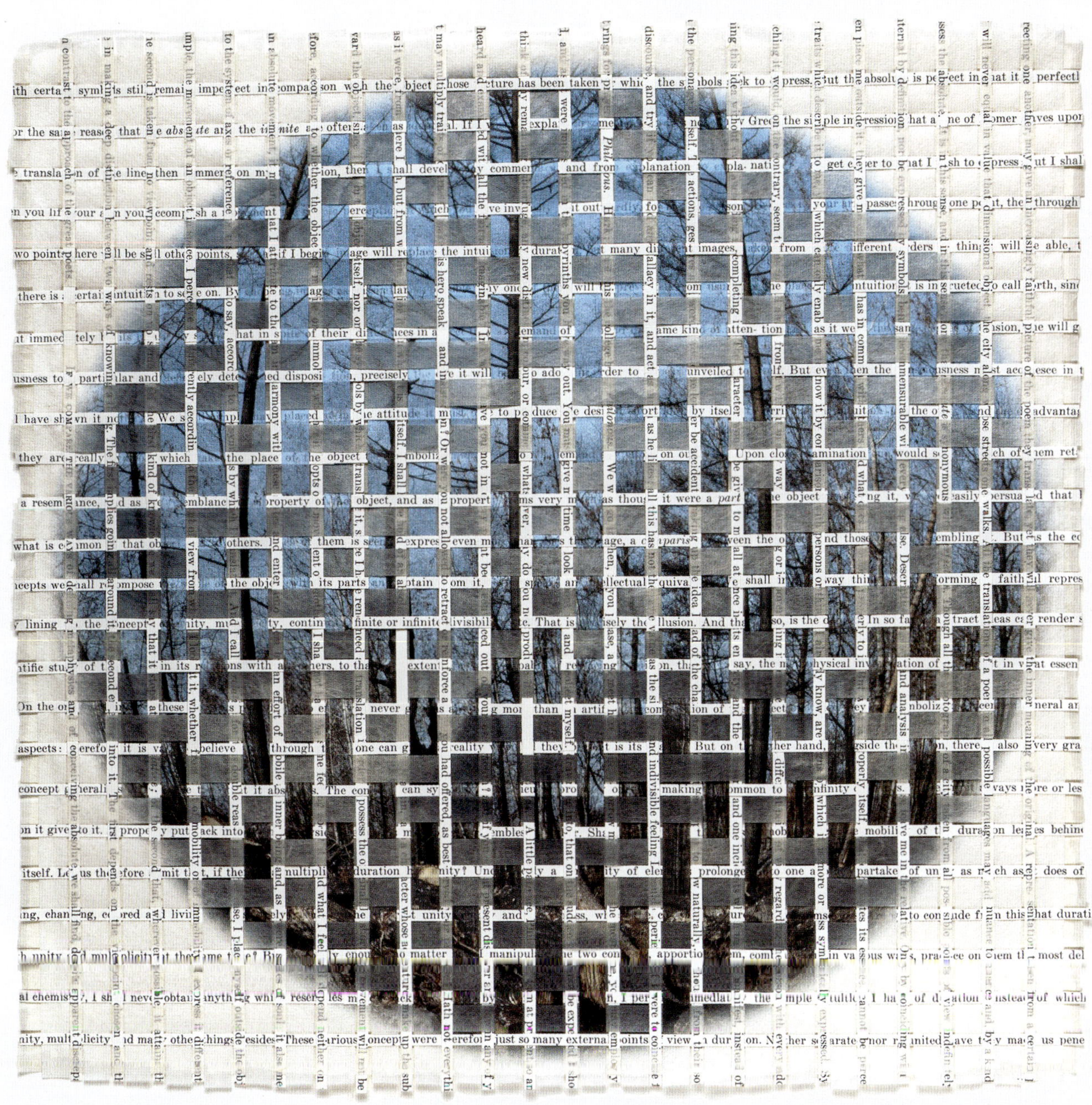

Mandala 8, by Therese Zemlin, 2023. 12" × 12", inkjet prints on Japanese paper, book pages, found text; weaving draft by Ralph Griswold, United States, 2005, #41493, from Handweaving.net. Book pages from *Philosophy: History and Problems* by Samuel E. Stumpf, 1971, and "Vital vs. Static Reality" by Henri Bergson. The photo of charred forest land was taken by the artist in 2021 near Greenwood Lake in northern Minnesota, soon after the Greenwood Fire. The photo of the clouds was taken in 2022.

Glossary

Since paper weaving is relatively new as an art form, some of these terms were invented for this book.

Note: An asterisk (*) before a glossary entry denotes a traditional cloth weaving term.

***interlacement:** The result of weaving warp and weft.

overweave: To weave additional elements into a basic weaving.

paper warp/paper loom: A piece of paper with parallel slits that are left intact on two edges. (See page 44.)

partial warp/partial loom: Similar to a paper warp/ paper loom, except only one edge is left intact.

***plain weave:** The most common weaving structure, in which the strips alternate: over one/under one, then under one/over one, and so on, to create an interlaced web.

strip weaving: A paper weaving in which both the warp and the weft are cut into strips that are then woven together.

***take-up:** The degree to which threads (in cloth weaving) or strips of paper (in paper weaving) bend (slightly) in order to travel over and/or under other strips to create the desired interlacement. Depending on the thickness of the paper you are weaving, take-up can cause a paper weaving to expand.

triaxial: A weaving with three sets of strips angled at 60 degrees to one another.

***twill:** A common weaving structure in which the weft strips go across the warp strips in a progression of interlacements to the right or left, forming a distinct diagonal pattern. Some of the strips in many twill interlacements travel over or under more than one strip. Twill structures include goose eye, herringbone, houndstooth, rosepath, and straight draw.

***warp:** A paper loom or (as in this book, unless otherwise noted) vertical strips in a paper strip weaving. In cloth weaving, the warp is composed of the threads that are stretched by and attached to the loom.

***weaving draft:** A diagram that shows how to interlace the paper warp and weft to create a specific weaving structure.

weaving structure: How the warp and weft strips interlace with each other (e.g., over/under/over/ under, over two/under one).

***weft:** A set of strips that are woven into the warp.

weft piece: A shaped piece of paper that will be cut into weft strips.

weft strip: An individual strip, which can be straight, curved, or shaped, that forms part of the weft.

woven section: The double layer that is created at each over/under juncture where two strips of paper overlap.

◀ *Interwoven Meditation*, by Susan L. Kristoferson, 2022. 32″ × 32″, artist-made hand-painted paste papers and purchased silver paper. Susan painted paste papers to get the colors, saturations, intensities, and textures needed to create the images in her mind. This collage, composed of woven paper sections, represents the Alberta, Canada, landscape that she could see from her home and studio, meditating on it every morning with a cup of tea as the sun rose.

Metric Conversion Chart

LENGTH		
To convert	To	Multiply
inches	millimeters	inches by 25.4
inches	centimeters	inches by 2.54
inches	meters	inches by 0.0254

US (inches)	Metric (centimeters)
0.5	1.27
1	2.54
1.5	3.81
2	5.08
2.5	6.35
3	7.62
3.5	8.89
4	10.16
4.5	11.43
5	12.70
5.5	13.97
6	15.24
6.5	16.51
7	17.78
7.5	19.05
8	20.32
8.5	21.59
9	22.86
9.5	24.13
10	25.40
11	27.94
12	30.48
13	33.02
14	35.56
15	38.10
16	40.64
17	43.18
18	45.72
19	48.26
20	50.80

Resources

Prompts and Templates

Download the list of 30 prompts and printable templates for projects in this book at storey.com/weaving-with-paper/.

Connect with Helen

Art, online classes, workshops: helenhiebertstudio.com

The Sunday Paper blog: helenhiebertstudio.com/blog

Paper Talk podcast: helenhiebertstudio.com/podcast

Facebook group: facebook.com/groups /HelenHiebertPaperStudio

Instagram: @helenhiebert

Weave Through Winter online class: helenhiebertstudio.com/weave-through-winter

The Paper Year membership: helenhiebertstudio.com /the-paper-year

Weaving Resources

Handweaving.net

Piglet's Potholder Patterns: potholders.piglet.org

Copyright-Free Images

loc.gov/free-to-use

unsplash.com

Paper Suppliers

Many local art supply stores carry a selection of decorative papers, and there are specialty paper stores in larger cities and online. Here are the websites for a few of my favorite shops.

Cambridge Imprint Patternmakers: cambridgeimprint.co.uk

Hiromi Paper Inc.: hiromipaper.com

Mulberry Paper & More: mulberrypaperandmore.com

Hollander's: hollanders.com/collections

Kozo Studio: kozo.studio

Origami-Shop: origami-shop.com

OrigamiUSA: origamiusa.org

Paper Connection International: paperconnection.com

Washi Arts: washiarts.com

Check out the longer list of paper shops in the Paper Advisor (helenhiebertstudio.com/the-paper-advisor), a page on my website that lists papermaking and papercraft resources, including information about tools and supplies, how-to videos, and paper tips—all in one place!

Suggested Reading

Specialty Supplies

Glue applicator: lampshop.com/product/glue-applicator-bottle

Weaving tool: washiarts.com/tools/long-metal-needle-tool-for-paper-weaving

PIT glue pen: washiarts.com/tools/fine-tip-japanese-pit-glue-pen

Sheet adhesive: washiarts.com/tools/double-sided-acid-free-premium-adhesive-tape

Armstrong, Rich. *The Perfect 100 Day Project: How to Choose, Make, and Finish Your Creative Project.* Rocky Nook, 2022.

Brosterman, Norman. *Inventing Kindergarten.* Harry N. Abrams, 1997.

Byrd, Susan J. *A Song of Praise for Shifu: Shifu Sanka.* Legacy Press, 2013.

Diehn, Gwen. *Live & Learn: Real Life Journals: Designing & Using Handmade Books.* Lark Books, 2010.

Jarchow, Deborah, and Gwen W. Steege. *The Weaving Explorer: Ingenious Techniques, Accessible Tools, and Creative Projects with Yarn, Paper, Wire, and More.* Storey Publishing, 2019.

Karuno, Hiroko. *Kigami and Kami-ito: Japanese Handmade Paper and Paper Thread.* Shikosha Publishing Co., 2017.

Kleon, Austin. *Steal Like an Artist: 10 Things Nobody Told You About Being Creative.* Workman Publishing, 2012.

LaPlantz, Shereen. *The Mad Weave Book: An Ancient Form of Triaxial Basket Weaving.* Dover Publications, Inc., 1984.

——. *Twill Basketry: A Handbook of Designs, Techniques, and Styles.* Lark Books, 1993.

Lee, Aimee. *Hanji Unfurled: One Journey into Korean Papermaking.* Legacy Press, 2012.

McGuinness, Dorothy. *The Art of Contemporary Woven Paper Basketry: Explorations in Diagonal Twill.* Schiffer Craft, 2021.

Schepper, Anna, and Lene Schepper. *The Art of Paper Weaving: 46 Colorful, Dimensional Projects.* Quarry Books, 2015.

Stanfield, Alyson. *I'd Rather Be in the Studio! The Artist's No-Excuse Guide to Self-Promotion.* Pentas Press, 2008.

Walker, Louisa. *Varied Occupations in Weaving.* Macmillan Company, 1901.

Wiebe, Edward. *Paradise of Childhood: A Practical Guide to Kindergartners*, Golden Jubilee ed. Milton Bradley Co., 1916.

Also by Helen Hiebert

The Art of Papercraft. Storey Publishing, 2022.

The Papermaker's Companion. Storey Publishing, 2000.

Papermaking with Garden Plants & Common Weeds. Storey Publishing, 2006.

Playing with Paper. Quarry Books, 2013.

Image List

Photographs by Mars Vilaubi unless otherwise noted.
Weavings by Helen Hiebert unless otherwise noted.

Chapter 1

p. 14. *Froebel Album*, year unknown, 8" x 6" x 1½"

p. 16. Plant-dyed handmade paper skeins, spun by Hiroko Karuno, 2012. 220 m/skein, handmade Japanese paper from Kadoide, Niigata Prefecture. Photograph by Kenji Maruyama.

p. 17. *Summer Robe (Jinbei)*, by Susan Byrd, 1986. 37½" × 41½", cotton warp and paper weft, three shades of indigo dye.

p. 18. *Teapot*, by Aimee Lee, 2014. 7¼" tall × 7" across spout, 3" base diameter, lacquer on corded and twined hanji.

p. 19. *Squaw*, by Shan Goshorn, 2018. 22¼" × 16¼" × 10½," arches watercolor paper splints printed with archival inks, artificial sinew, and copper frame. Photograph courtesy of the Virginia Museum of Fine Arts, Richmond. Funds provided by Margaret A. and C. Boyd Clarke and Mareke Schiller, 2021.191.

p. 20. *Froebel Album*, year unknown. 8" × 6" × 1½".

p. 23. *Heart-and-Hand Love Token*, artist unidentified, 1840–1860. 12" × 14", ink and varnish on cut paper. Photograph by John Parnell.

p. 23. Untitled work by Mary Balzer Buskirk, 1968. 36" × 24", wool and nylon with twigs. Reproduced with permission of the estate of Mary Balzer Buskirk.

Chapter 2

p. 27. *Hiding in Plain Sight #6: Relics*, by Audrey L. Pinto, 2023. 132" × 48". Photograph by Will Howcroft Photography.

p. 28. *Garden*, by Lisa Merkin, Weave Through Winter (WTW) online class 2021. 7½" × 9", textured pebble paper, packaging material, Canson Mi-Teintes paper.

p. 29. *Egg Basket*, by Helen Hiebert, 2021. 11" × 12".

p. 30. *Smock*, by Helen Hiebert, 2023. 11" × 8½", inkjet print, decorative paper.

Chapter 3

p. 42. Untitled work by Kristi Galbraith, WTW 2022. Approximately 12" × 9", assorted papers.

p. 51. *River Strata*, by Amanda Thackray, 2023. 32" × 22½", woven artist-made paper. Photograph by Kevin Frances.

p. 53. *Going in Circles*, by Lisa Bayne Astor, WTW 2023. 6¼" × 7", inkjet print of artist's original painting, plus text on copier paper.

p. 55. Untitled works by Cathy Moore, WTW 2024.

p. 56. *Culture*, by Laurel (Laurie) Moorhead, WTW 2022. 5¼" × 7¾".

Chapter 4

p. 60. *Holding On*, by Wendy Rochman, WTW 2024. 8" × 6½", magazine pages.

p. 63. *Quarterdeck*, by Gina Pisello, 2023. 6⅛" × 4", vintage file folder, silhouette paper, vintage silhouettes, gold origami paper, black lokta paper, numbers and letters typed on vintage Underwood portable typewriter, rubber-stamped letters and numbers.

p. 65. *Fore/Back: Ground*, by Janice Mcdonald, 2019. 12" × 9", collage on watercolor paper (collage reproduction serves as warp with collected papers as weft).

p. 67. *Paper Weavings*, by Rebecca Winter, WTW 2021–2023. 9¼" × 7½" × 2½", coffee-dyed mixed-media art paper, Coptic handwoven cover fabric made on a floor loom using cotton and novelty synthetic yarns.

Chapter 5

Weaving 1: Recycle

p. 75. Untitled work by Cathy Moore, WTW 2023. 7½" × 5¼", two chocolate bar wrappers.

p. 75. *Bread Essentials*, by Judy Jacques, WTW 2023. 6¼" × 5½", King Arthur bread flour bags.

Weaving 2: Roots

p. 77. Untitled work by Cathleen Higgins, WTW 2023. 8⅜" × 8¼", Japanese shibori origami paper, Nature Conservancy calendar page featuring tree roots.

p. 77. *Rootless*, by Terry Englehart, WTW 2023. 8" × 11", South Carolina road atlas pages, mileage chart.

Weaving 3: Joy

p. 81. *Joy*, by Carol Ann Waugh, WTW 2023. 13" × 7", artist-made paper, black strips cut from a book page.

p. 81. *Garden Grid*, by Helen Hiebert, WTW 2021. 6" × 10½", decorative Japanese paper and Tant origami papers.

Weaving 4: World

p. 84. *Europe*, by Carol Ann Waugh, WTW 2023. 10" × 8", book pages from a world atlas, toothpicks, flags from Portugal, Spain, France, Italy, and the United Kingdom.

p. 85. *Marriage of Two Minds*, by Indira Govindan, WTW 2023. 10" × 8", wrapping paper, newspaper pages.

Weaving 5: Nature

p. 87. Untitled work by Kristi Galbraith, WTW 2023. 10" × 10", Japanese woodblock-print origami papers.

p. 87. *Blossom*, by Davida Feder, WTW 2023. 8½" × 7⅜", copier paper.

Weaving 6: Travel

p. 89. *Airport Tags*, by Denise Marshall, WTW 2023. 8½" × 12¼", matte photo paper, airport tags, string.

p. 89. Untitled work by Diane K. Bauerle, WTW 2023. 8" × 8", paper receipts, sewing thread.

Weaving 7: Landscape

p. 91. *Mountaintop*, by Helen Hiebert, WTW 2020. 11" × 8½", Thai banana/banana mash paper, gold leaf print.

p. 91. *Home*, by Robin Kessler, WTW 2024. 7¼" × 6", light cardstock in four colors.

Weaving 8: Random

p. 93. *Heart in (Gloved) Hand*, by Kirilka Stavreva, WTW 2023. 8½" × 5", decorative paper.

p. 93. *Woven Blooms*, by Michelle May, WTW 2023. 12" × 3", black and handmade Indian cotton paper.

Weaving 9: Contrast

p. 96. Untitled work by Sarah Morgan, WTW 2024. 15" × 11", part of a black-and-white painting found at a recycling center, red textured cardstock.

p. 97. *The Same Side of the Street*, by Denise Marshall, WTW 2023. 17½" × 15", Hahnemühle Museum Etching cotton paper.

Weaving 10: Perspective

p. 99. *The Barbie-fication of Yosemite Valley*, by Ron Shaull, WTW 2024. 8" × 10", photograph used in weaving taken by Ron, pink 65 lb cardstock.

p. 99. *Room with a View*, by Patricia Minard, WTW 2023. 6" × 6", lightweight cardstock, magazine page.

Weaving 11: Routine

p. 103. *Wall in the Woods*, by Cynthia Reid, WTW 2023. 8½" × 11".

p. 103. Untitled work by Karen Hall, WTW 2023. 4¼" × 7½", copier paper, deli paper, acrylic paint.

Weaving 12: Window

p. 106. *View*, by Davida Feder, WTW 2022. 8⅜" × 5¾", copier paper.

p. 107. Untitled work by Cynthia Reid, WTW 2023. 10" × 7", illustration and music from a vintage children's songbook, chiyogami.

Weaving 13: Direction

p. 110. *Points de suture (Medical Stitches)*, by Héloïse Bossard, WTW 2024. Approximately 7" × 8", diagonal text strips woven into chiyogami paper.

p. 111. *Captured in the Weave*, by Beverly Frey, WTW 2024. 11½" × 9", ombré cardstock.

Weaving 14: Circle

p. 115. *On Target*, by Susan Buhler-Maki, WTW 2023. 9" diameter, scrapbook paper.

p. 115. Untitled work by Héloïse Bossard, WTW 2024. 6¼" × 4¾", parchment paper, printed kraft paper.

Weaving 15: Concentric

p. 119. Untitled work by Ron Shaull, WTW 2024. 5½" × 5½", red 65 lb cardstock, wallpaper remnant.

p. 119. *Tunnel*, by Helen Hiebert, WTW 2023. 6" × 6", lacquered Japanese paper, Pearlized Grasses decorative paper.

Weaving 16: Ephemera

p. 123. Untitled work by Cathy Moore, WTW 2023. 7½" × 5¼", artist-made paper.

p. 123. *Iowa Fox*, by Kirilka Stavreva, WTW 2023. 6¼" × 11", Indian crinkle paper, calendar page, copper wire.

Weaving 17: Silhouette

p. 127. *Raku*, by Shirley Cook, WTW 2024. 7¼" × 5¼", acrylic paint on inkjet and laser paper.

p. 127. Untitled work by Rebecca Winter, WTW 2023. 8⅛" × 8¼", image printed on 90 gsm banana paper, red kraft paper of about the same weight.

Weaving 18: Highlight

p. 131. *Cat Eyes*, by Susan Buhler-Maki, WTW 2023. 9" × 8", cardstock, 90 lb watercolor paper.

p. 131. Untitled work by Karen Hall, 2023. 8½" × 5¾", copier paper, purchased paper, music paper, acrylic paint.

Weaving 19: Symbol

p. 133. *Dove*, by Helen Hiebert, WTW 2024. 6" × 7¾", Tant origami paper, Japanese chiyogami paper.

p. 133. Untitled work by Cathy Moore, WTW 2023. 5½" × 7½", three contrasting papers.

Weaving 20: Winding

p. 135. Untitled work by Therese Lennert, WTW 2024. 8" × 8", paper, monotype.

p. 135. *Succulent Spiral*, by Lisa Merkin, WTW 2021. 8" diameter, image of *Aloe polyphylla*, momigami paper, marbled paper.

Weaving 21: Crossing

p. 138. *Caning Memories*, by Judy Jacques, WTW 2023. 9½" × 8½", fluorescent paper, pre-cut strips.

p. 139. Untitled work by Kristi Galbraith, WTW 2024. 4" × 3", woven papers mounted on a 7" × 5" card.

Weaving 22: Treasure

p. 143. *Stepping Out*, by Meredith Johanson, WTW 2024. 7½" × 7¾", pattern-printed paper, gold paper.

p. 143. *Rolling PinDemic*, by Karen Krieger, 2022. 5½" × 22" × 5½", artist-made papers, vintage text, archival backing paper, embroidery floss, wooden dowel. Photograph by David Montgomery, courtesy of Karen Krieger.

Weaving 23: Waves

p. 148. *Japanese Clouds*, by Héloïse Bossard, WTW 2024. 6" × 6", chiyogami, gray Japanese paper.

p. 149. Untitled work by Sarah Morgan, WTW 2024. 3" × 4½", blue glitter paper woven into an architectural drawing, photocopied onto paper with suminagashi marbling.

Weaving 24: Light

p. 153. *Step Into the Light*, by Helen Hiebert, 2025. 9" x 9", artist-made abaca paper, decorative paper.

p. 153. *Life Finds a Way*, by Beverly Frey, WTW 2022. 11" × 9", ombré scrapbook paper.

Weaving 25: Layer

p. 155. *View out the Window*, by Meredith Johanson, WTW 2024. 6¾" × 6¾", origami papers.

p. 155. *Autumn, Dancing*, by Suellen Meyer, WTW 2024. 6" × 6", printed origami paper, decorative paper.

Weaving 26: Variety

p. 157. *Gridlock*, by Helen Hiebert, WTW 2024. 11" × 8½", assorted decorative and artist-made papers.

p. 157. *Cattywampus*, by Robin Kessler, WTW 2024. 8½" × 7½", various papers left over from a month of weaving, including metallic cover stock, LaCroix package, text from a book of fairy tales, calendar pages, and marble-patterned paper.

Weaving 27: Modular

p. 161. *Waiting*, by Arlene Brenner, WTW 2023. 10¾" × 8½", copy of original pen-and-ink drawing, gold metallic pen, Strathmore black canvas paper, hand-painted collage paper, DMC black cotton pearl embroidery thread.

p. 161. *Echo Park and Me*, by Susan W. Melczer, WTW 2021. 7½" × 7½", Japanese chiyogami paper woven into a reproduction of *Echo Park*, 2016, by photographer George Byrne from his book *Post Truth*, 2020.

Weaving 28: Breathe

p. 163. *Waves and Angles*, by Patricia Minard, WTW 2023. 7" × 5", 80 lb blank greeting card, origami paper.

p. 163. Untitled work by Marguerite Katchen, WTW 2024. Artist-made and amate bark papers.

Weaving 29: Angle

p. 165. *Where the Light Shines*, by Hilarie Rath, WTW 2023. 8½" × 8½", two sheets of origami paper.

p. 165. *Concentric*, by Helen Hiebert, WTW 2024. 9" × 9", Japanese linen papers.

Weaving 30: Puzzle

p. 172. *Wild Flowers in a Vase*, by Davida Feder, WTW 2024. 8" × 5¾", copier paper.

p. 172. *BlueGreenRed*, by Beverly Frey, 2024. 9" × 11", decorative papers.

p. 173. *Stars and Diamonds*, by Gina Pisello, WTW 2024. 6" × 5¼", hand-marbled paper, Italian Kartos paper, artist's tape to hold strips in place on back.

p. 173. *Foundation*, by Therese Lennert, WTW 2024. 4" × 4", linocut on Japanese paper with triaxial paper weaving, using a monotype print.

Chapter 6

p. 183. *Gewebte Reflexionen (Woven Reflections)*, by Kristi Galbraith, 2023. 8½" × 10½" × 1", 10 pages + cover; outer cover and inner "frame" pages are cover-weight dark brown and natural; smooth burgundy; and felt-finish khaki.

Chapter 7: Gallery

Hollie Chastain

p. 190. *Psychopomp I*, by Hollie Chastain, 2018. 6" × 6", paper, thread.

p. 191. *Psychopomp II*, by Hollie Chastain, 2018. 6" × 6", paper, thread.

p. 191. *Psychopomp III*, by Hollie Chastain, 2019. 7" × 7", paper.

Galen Gibson-Cornell

p. 192. *Queen*, by Galen Gibson-Cornell, 2022. 53" × 59", found street posters from Sofia, Bulgaria, sliced and woven. Photo courtesy of Galen Gibson-Cornell.

p. 192. *Montagne Flambée (Flaming Mountain)*, by Galen Gibson-Cornell, 2022. 60" × 40" × 4", found street posters from New York City, sliced and woven. Photo courtesy of Galen Gibson-Cornell.

p. 193. *Aerial*, by Galen Gibson-Cornell, 2022. 78" × 110", found street posters from Berlin, Germany; Plovdiv and Sofia, Bulgaria; Buenos Aires, Argentina; New York City and Philadelphia; Venice, Italy; sliced and woven. Photo courtesy of Galen Gibson-Cornell.

p. 193. Galen Gibson-Cornell in his Philadelphia studio. Photo courtesy of Galen Gibson-Cornell.

p. 194–195. *Aerial* (detail). Photo courtesy of Galen Gibson-Cornell.

Naomi J. Kendall

p. 196. *Binca Blue*, by Naomi J. Kendall, 2023. Approximately 16½" × 11¾", woven paper.

p. 196. *Strata*, by Naomi J. Kendall, 2021. Approximately 29½" × 27½", woven paper. Photo by Naomi J. Kendall.

p. 197. *Latitude*, by Naomi J. Kendall, 2021. Approximately 21¾" × 20¾", woven paper. Photo by Naomi J. Kendall.

Carole Kunstadt

p. 198. *Sacred Poem LXVII*, by Carole Kunstadt, 2010. 9" × 9", nylon thread, gold leaf, paper—pages from *Parish Psalmody,* dated 1849 (504 knots). Photo by Kevin Kunstadt.

p. 198. *Sacred Poem LXXXIX*, by Carole Kunstadt, 2014. 5" × 6½" × 2½". 24-karat gold leaf, interfacing, paper—pages from *Parish Psalmody,* dated 1849. Photo by Kevin Kunstadt.

p. 199. *Interlude No. 23*, by Carole Kunstadt, 2021. 8¼" × 8½", thread, oak gall ink on paper—nineteenth-century music manuscripts published by Dantier/Paris. Photo by Carole Kunstadt.

Dorothy McGuinness

p. 200. *Shooting Stars*, by Dorothy McGuinness, 2019. 9" × 12" × 10", watercolor paper, acrylic paint, waxed linen thread. Photo by Dorothy McGuinness.

p. 200. *Byzantine*, by Dorothy McGuinness, 2019. 9" × 20" × 14", watercolor paper, acrylic paint, polyester thread. Photo by Dorothy McGuinness.

p. 201. *Variation on a Theme 4*, by Dorothy McGuinness, 2022. 8" × 14" × 9", watercolor paper, acrylic paint, waxed linen thread. Photo by Dorothy McGuinness.

Rhiannon "Skye" Tafoya

p. 202. *Contraction*, by Rhiannon "Skye" Tafoya, 2021. 15¾" × 17", Colorplan papers. Photo by Aaron Paden.

p. 203. *Rhythmic*, by Rhiannon "Skye" Tafoya, 2021. 14" × 11", screen print woven with a screen print. Photo by Aaron Paden.

Julie VonDerVellen

p. 204. *Bright Side*, by Julie VonDerVellen, 2022. 8½" × 8½", artist-made paper, watercolor.

p. 205. *Date Due: Withdrawn*, by Julie VonDerVellen, 2022. 6¼" × 12½", artist-made paper, recycled library date-due cards.

p. 205. *Checking In*, by Julie VonDerVellen, 2022. 11½" × 7⅛", artist-made paper, acrylic.

Therese Zemlin

p. 206. *The Last Drop: Rocks and Water*, by Therese Zemlin, 2021. 11" × 13", inkjet prints on Japanese paper, book pages; weaving draft by Ivo Kastanak, Austria, 1903, from Handweaving.net. Book pages from Rachel Carson's *Silent Spring*. Photo by Therese Zemlin.

p. 207. *Mandala 8*, by Therese Zemlin, 2023. 12" × 12", inkjet prints on Japanese paper, book pages, found text; weaving draft by Ralph Griswold, United States, 2005, #41493, from Handweaving.net. Book pages from *Philosophy: History and Problems*, by Samuel Enoch Stumpf. "Vital Versus Static Reality," Henri Bergson (*Introduction to Metaphysics*), pp. 336–46, McGraw Hill, 1971. Photo by Jack Mader.

Back Matter

p. 208. *Interwoven Meditation*, by Susan L. Kristoferson, 2022. 32" × 32", artist-made hand-painted paste papers and purchased silver paper. Photo by Susan L. Kristoferson.

Contributing Artists

Astor, Lisa Bayne (page 53): @lisabayne

Bauerle, Diane K. (page 89): @bauerlediane

Bossard, Héloïse (pages 110, 115, 148): audetourdupapier.com; @audetourdupapier

Brenner, Arlene (page 161)

Buhler-Maki, Susan (pages 115, 131): @suebuhmak

Buskirk, Mary Balzer (page 23)

Byrd, Susan (page 17)

Chastain, Hollie (pages 190–191): holliechastain.com

Cook, Shirley (page 127): @jumpdogmom

Englehart, Terry (page 77)

Feder, Davida (pages 87, 106, 172): @dfeder3

Frey, Beverly (pages 111, 153, 172)

Galbraith, Kristi (pages 42, 87, 139, 183): @kristigalbraith

Gibson-Cornell, Galen (pages 192–194): galengibsoncornell.com

Goshorn, Shan (page 19)

Govindan, Indira (page 85): @indiragovi

Hall, Karen (pages 103, 131): @karen55hall

Hiebert, Helen (pages 29, 30, 82, 91, 119, 133, 157, 165)

Higgins, Cathleen (page 77)

Jacques, Judy (pages 75, 138)

Johanson, Meredith (pages 143, 155): @meredithjohansonart

Karuno, Hiroko (page 16)

Katchen, Marguerite (page 163)

Kendall, Naomi J. (pages 196–197): naomijkendall.com

Kessler, Robin (pages 91, 157): @rk4889

Krieger, Karen (page 143): karenkrieger.com; @kkmetals

Kristoferson, Susan L. (page 224): kristoferson-studio.ca

Kunstadt, Carole (pages 198–199): carolekunstadt.com

Lee, Aimee (page 18): aimeelee.net

Lennert, Therese (pages 135, 173): centrechatbleu.com/artists/lennert; @mahofo.prints

Marshall, Denise (pages 89, 97): denisejillmarshall.com; @denisejillmarshall

May, Michelle (page 93): theraspberryrabbits.com; @theraspberryrabbits

McDonald, Janice (page 65): janicemcdonald.com

McGuinness, Dorothy (pages 200–201): dorothymmcguinness.com

Melczer, Susan (page 161)

Merkin, Lisa (pages 28, 135): lisamerkinart.com; @bookartistlisam

Meyer, Suellen (page 155)

Minard, Patricia (pages 99, 163)

Moore, Cathy (pages 55, 75, 123, 133)

Moorhead, Laurel (Laurie; page 56): @lauriemoorhead

Morgan, Sarah (pages 96, 149)

Pinto, Audrey L. (page 27): @audreypintoart

Pisello, Gino (pages 63, 173): ginapisello.com; @gina_pisello

Rath, Hilarie (page 165): @rathhilarie

Reid, Cynthia (pages 103, 107, 153)

Rochman, Wendy (page 60)

Shaull, Ron (pages 99, 119): @zenpaparon

Stavreva, Kirilka (pages 93, 123): @kat.stav

Tafoya, Rhiannon "Skye" (pages 202–203): skyetafoya.com

Thackray, Amanda (page 51): ajthackray.com; @mandattacks

VonDerVellen, Julie (pages 204–205): julievondervellen.com

Waugh, Carol Ann (pages 81, 84): CarolAnnWaugh.com; @carolannwaugh3

Winter, Rebecca (pages 67, 127): @rebeccawinter555

Zemlin, Therese (pages 206–207): theresezemlin.com

Acknowledgments

I am eternally grateful to the following people who helped make this book so much richer than it would have been if I had taken this as a solo journey:

Lisa Merkin attended my first few Weave Through Winter online classes and suggested that I start using prompts to spark ideas for the daily weavings. This has become a highly anticipated element, and Lisa has come up with thematic prompts for the course since 2020. She also crafted the longer prompts for this book. Lisa, you are a delight to mince words with. And, readers, I hope the prompts will encourage you, guide you, and maybe even keep you up at night (with excitement).

Rebecca Winter is a handweaver who has participated in several sessions of Weave Through Winter, and she has been instrumental in helping me understand the overlapping aspects of paper and cloth weaving. She also reviewed parts of this book and assisted in writing the glossary. We had to invent some terms!

Beverly Frey is also a regular Weave Through Winter participant. She is an innovative weaving structure designer and integrates technology into her process. Bev encouraged me to persist on my journey as I struggled to master triaxial weaving by putting together a set of instructions that I was able to follow. My instructions (on page 166) were developed from her initial work. Bev uses Adobe Illustrator to create digital warp and weft files, which she then overlaps to predict how a weaving will look; she also uses a Silhouette cutting machine to create intricate paper pieces. She even designed a program (with the assistance of her son) to determine the outcome of various strip-color combinations in the triaxial weave.

Alyson Stanfield, who runs Art Biz Success, has helped me tremendously over the years with the business and marketing side of my practice, as well as integrating my art and programs into community building.

Special thanks to the team at Storey: to Deborah Balmuth, for believing that all five of my books should come to life; to my project editor, Kristen Hewitt, for finessing the manuscript, keeping me on task, and staying calm and collected throughout the editing process; to Mars Vilaubi, for the wonderful photos—I enjoyed working with you; and to Alee Moncy and the publicity team—it is wonderful to have assistance in getting my books out into the world.

I have featured many innovative paper weavers throughout the pages of this book, but I know I have missed a few! You are included in my thanks.

Index

Page numbers in italics indicate photos or illustrations.

About the Author

Helen Hiebert is a Colorado artist who constructs installations, sculptures, films, artists' books, and works in paper using handmade paper as her primary medium. She teaches, lectures, and exhibits her work internationally and online and is the author of several how-to books about papermaking and papercrafts, including *The Art of Papercraft*, *Playing with Paper*, and *Papermaking with Garden Plants & Common Weeds*. Helen has an extensive network of paper colleagues around the world, and her interest in how things are made (from paper) keeps her up-to-date on current paper trends, which she writes about in her weekly blog, *The Sunday Paper*. She interviews papermakers and paper artists on her podcast *Paper Talk*, and she holds an annual paper retreat and papermaking master classes in her Red Cliff studio.